1435
North Oakland Blvd
Williams
48237

Unless otherwise indicated, all Scripture quotations are taken from the *King James Version* (KJV) of the Bible.

All rights reserved. No portion of this book may be reproduced, stored in a retrieval system, or transmitted in any form or by any means – electronic, mechanical, photocopy, recording, scanning, or otherwise – without prior written permission of the author.

Transcribed by Diane Narlock

Contributing Editors: Susan Wahid and Brad Shirley

Copyright © 2015 Dr. Leonard Gardner
All rights reserved.
ISBN-10: 1502716577
ISBN-13: 978-1502716576

AFTER ME, YOU'RE FIRST!

Dealing with Self

By

Dr. Leonard Gardner

2015

Contents

Acknowledgement..vii
Chapter 1 - Introductions and Definitions 1
Chapter 2 - The Origin...17
Chapter 3 - The Mixture...27
Chapter 4 - Counseling..45
Chapter 5 - An Important Triad....................................57
Chapter 6 - Battle for the Throne.................................69
Chapter 7 - Embracing The Cross...............................83

Acknowledgement

In the 1990's, a book entitled "The Kingdom Cult of Self" written by Kevin Conner, a man of God whom I highly esteem, found its way into my hands from an unknown source. It was one of those occurrences of divine providence, not only because of its timeliness, but because it contained many thoughts I had repeatedly woven into many of the messages I had preached prior to that time. As I read the book, I became glued to each page. It witnessed with my spirit to such a degree that I remember hearing myself repeatedly exclaiming "Amen!" and even occasionally being brought to tears of joy with the words "Praise God!"

I am convinced that many in the church world, including some leaders, mistakenly believe that the Holy Spirit comes to dwell within us for the purpose of *changing* our sinful nature to be more Christ-like. However, Scripture clearly teaches that our sinful nature must be *"put to death."* Such action occurred *judicially* at Calvary but must take place *experientially* as we daily *die to self* (I Corinthians 15:31) so that the life of Christ may be lived through us by the power of the Holy Spirit.

Giving Kevin Conner due credit while using parts of his book alongside other contrary but popular secular material on self-esteem, and driven by my deeply established convictions, I developed an eight-week course which I taught to my congregation approximately twenty years ago. The teaching was recorded on audio tape and subsequently transcribed to hard copy. A relatively short time ago, we decided to publish this teaching, with Kevin Conner's permission, under the title "After Me, You're First!"

It is my sincere prayer that with an open ear and a teachable spirit, every reader will hear and be spiritually blessed and strengthened in our pursuit of a victorious Christian life for the glory of God.

Chapter 1

Introductions and Definitions

We hear much about the kingdom of God as well as the kingdom of darkness. Jesus brought a message that was carried on by the Apostle Paul which teaches us something I am calling *After Me, You're First! Dealing with Self*. Self must be recognized and dealt with in each of our lives. If we do not deal with "self," it will keep us from experiencing the full manifestation of God's intended purpose for our lives. Jesus could never have gone to the cross unless He had dealt with self in Gethsemane. He was in a battle between His human will and the Father's will. Jesus won the battle when He said, "Not My will, but Thine be done" (Luke 22:42). There is an ongoing battle for the throne of your life as well. Self wants to be the focus, but God wants and deserves to be on the throne. You make the ultimate choice of which king sits on the throne of your life and which kingdom you will embrace. Creating a kingdom of self by putting self on the throne is prelude to disaster. Scripture teaches that our lives should be God-centered. God is to be on the throne, not self. We have to deal with self. In this book, we will learn how to do that.

I am convinced that God wants His people to be able to clearly discern the truth. The Word of God declares that the truth will make us free (John 8:32), and by the Holy Spirit we can know truth and separate it from error. There is much error in the world today, and we need to be able to properly divide the Word of Truth.

Over the years as a pastor, I have asked God to help me to come to a greater understanding of how to help people, including myself, mature in the things of God and come to places of greater effectiveness, fruitfulness, and anointing. I feel that is one of the major responsibilities of a pastor, and it is therefore my desire to be an instrument in the hand of God to that end. There are reasons why, in some cases, people stagnate. They simply crystallize and don't mature in God. However, Hebrews 6:1 clearly calls us to go on to maturity, which literally means perfection, completion, and fulfillment. I believe it is important that we ask the Lord the reasons why we stagnate. "Lord, is there something that I am missing? Is there something in my life that I have overlooked? Is there something to which I am not paying proper attention? Are my priorities right? What is it, Lord?" We each have a destiny, and I want to see it fulfilled in each of our lives. We must search our own hearts and ask God for the grace to see and understand the things that may be obstacles or hindrances along the way. He who has already determined our destiny, ordained us, created us, and called us, is wholly committed to reveal these things to us. It is consistent with His nature and His desire.

Dangerous Times

Paul was mentoring Timothy and preparing him to be a pastor in the New Testament church. The things that Paul writes in his Epistles, including those to Timothy, apply not only to pastors but to all of us who seek to come to the full manifestation of God's intended purpose. Second Timothy 3:1 says, "This know also that in the last days, perilous times shall come." The word "perilous" means dangerous. I believe that we would all agree we are living in dangerous times.

In the list of dangerous things in 2 Timothy 3:2-4, I am amazed the Lord didn't talk about the things that we consider most dangerous today. I am sure He was aware that crime would increase in these days. I am sure He was aware that weapons would exist with the capability of wiping out millions of people. But the Word of God calls our attention, instead, to altogether different things – things dealing with self. Paul declares, first of all, "Men shall be lovers of their own selves" and because of that, they would be "covetous, boasters, proud, blasphemers, disobedient to parents, unthankful, unholy, without natural affection, trucebreakers, false accusers, incontinent [unrestrained or uncontrolled], fierce, despisers of those who are good, traitors, heady, high-minded, lovers of pleasure more than lovers of God." Seeking after pleasure, and the conviction that pleasure is the fulfillment needed to make a life complete, is called *hedonism*. God is not saying that there would be lovers of pleasure *rather* than lovers of God, but He says *more than*. He is not talking about replacement but degree.

Second Timothy 3:5-7 continues, "Having a form of godliness, but denying the power thereof: from such turn away. For of this sort are they which creep into houses, and lead captive silly women laden with sins, led away with divers lusts, ever learning, and never able to come to the knowledge of the truth." Verse 13 declares, "Evil men and seducers shall wax worse and worse, deceiving and being deceived." This entire list begins with an evil kind of self-love, and all of these other things come out of that sinful self-love in this hedonistic society. People who love pleasure more than they love God are a prominent part of this list.

Humanism and the New Age

In this book, we will examine things that are part of the ungodly philosophy called *humanism*, which is so rampant in the world today. Of equal danger is the entire New Age movement. Most Christians, if asked whether they believe in humanism or New Age philosophy, will immediately say, "Of course not." Many times we respond in this way simply because we have heard someone say it's not godly or scriptural, but we really don't know what it is. We don't know why it's not godly and not scriptural. God isn't interested in us simply taking a negative position against a word. He wants us to understand the deceitfulness and deceptiveness of evil and sin so that we are able to rise up quickly against it and to declare, "This is not the Word of the Lord, it is not the way of the Lord, and, therefore, I will not embrace it as a part of my life."

First Corinthians 10:1 states, "Moreover, brethren, I would not that ye should be ignorant." In addition to addressing several things which are somewhat obvious, we will address other issues, that may appear to be more subtle, yet which I believe are keeping many Christians from living in victory. One of these is the philosophy of self-actualization, which is sort of an umbrella that covers and includes such things as the tremendous emphasis today on self-esteem. I intend to show you from the Word of God that some things being preached from pulpits, as well as on television, are not scriptural and are deadly to the Christian life.

If you look under "self" in Webster's dictionary, you may be surprised to find that there are about 130 words that begin with the word "self." I have listed a number of them here, extracted directly from the dictionary: self-abuse, self-admiration, self-advancement, self-aggrandizement, self-annihilation, self-applause, self-appointed, self-appreciation, self-approbation, self-assertion, self-beguiling, self-blinded, self-conceited, self-concerned, self-confidence, self-congratulation, self-conservation, self-content, self-centered, self-contempt, self-consumed, self-complacent, self-deceived, self-defense, self-deluded, self-dependence, self-destruction, self-depraved, self-depreciation, self-despair, self-determine, self-discovery, self-expression, self-exaggeration, self-exaltation, self-fulfillment, self-flattery, self-glorification, self-gratification, self-hardening, self-help, self-hypnosis, self-idolize, self-importance, self-improvement, self-indulgent, self-introspection, selfishness, self-justification, self-murder, self-occupation, self-opinionated, self-pity, self-pleasing, self-power, self-praise, self-preference, self-preservation, self-pride, self-proclamation, self-protection, self-realization, self-reliance, self-repulsive, self-righteous, self-ruined, self-rule, self-seeking, self-style, self-sufficient, self-tormented, self-trust, and self-willed. Welcome to the kingdom of self, where self sits on the throne, and self is king.

No Compromise

I believe, for the most part, all of us who are committed to the Lord Jesus Christ are opposed to anything to which He is opposed. When we love the Lord and we know that He has taken a position against something, we are willing to take that same stand. However, part of what we deal with in this age is a very subtle way of diluting truth to the point that it isn't easily recognized. "Syncretism" is a word that is sometimes used. It speaks of mixture. It speaks of taking things that are actually opposites in principle and trying to combine them together to produce a kind of "soup" that is palatable and tasty to both believers and nonbelievers. Even in the religious world, we have endeavored to do the same thing to a great extent, through our own ecumenical efforts. We have followed paths of compromise to the point that truth has often been sacrificed for the sake of agreement. I am not in any way proposing division, but neither do we have the right to add one word or take one word away from Scripture (Revelation 22:19).

If God has crossed a *t*, it remains eternally crossed and if He has dotted an *i*, it remains eternally dotted. If someone doesn't like it, they should deal with that at the cross, not at the negotiating table. We must be careful that we understand the Word of the Lord to the extent that we will not be deceived.

Paul wrote to the New Testament church at Colossae (as recorded beginning in Colossians 2:6) and declared, "As ye have, therefore, received Christ Jesus the Lord, so walk ye in him." We are to be "rooted and built up in Him." "Rooted" speaks of going down and anchoring ourselves. "Built-up" speaks of growing and maturing. Both directions are essential to the mature Christian life. We are to be "established in the faith, as ye have been taught, abounding therein with thanksgiving." Notice verse 8, "Beware lest any man spoil you through philosophy and vain deceit, after the tradition of men, after the rudiments of the world, and not after Christ." Please take note of the word "any." Deception can come from "anywhere" and/or "anyone." Beware that no one *spoils* you meaning that no one takes you captive, that you do not become a prisoner of philosophy and vain deceit. Paul is saying it is important that you do not have bad roots. Be constantly looking and keeping a watchful eye. The word "spoil" in the Greek means "to carry off as a captive or a slave." Beware that you are not carried away by something that is not of God.

The word "philosophy" isn't a bad word in and of itself. It's the *kind* of philosophy that is important for us to discern. Philosophy, by definition, is "a group of beliefs, concepts, or attitudes that form a certain mentality, position, or conviction." Philosophy comes to us from many influences. We must be wary of what voices to which we listen, and what we receive. The Lord has made it very clear to me that there is a difference between having something spoken *unto* you as opposed to spoken *into* you. We can't always control what is spoken *unto* us, but we *can* control what's spoken *into* us. In other words, we are watchmen of our own hearts. You don't have to let everybody speak *into* your life. Personally, I am careful about who speaks *into* my life, though many people speak *unto* my life. Consider this illustration: you can't always control who comes to your front door (*unto* your house), but you can control who comes *into* your house. Any collection of beliefs, concepts, attitudes, and convictions, must be measured in the light of Scripture. Be careful about what you let into your life!

Led by the Spirit

I am wary of people that overuse the phrase "led by the Spirit" or "hearing from the Spirit" because it can be a very subjective thing. If what we are hearing is not confirmed in the Word, then we must check our hearing. Simply saying "the Spirit told me" doesn't make it true. It's important to hear this, because there are key phrases and key words that cause some people to open their spiritual door. When I was in the business world, we would get into heated discussions, and I was amused by the techniques that people would use to get their point across. There was one man in particular who would stand up and pound the table with his fist as hard as he could, curse repeatedly, and then "reiterate" his point. He went through all of those actions and motions to get doors open.

God certainly reveals things by His Spirit, and He works by His Spirit. We live by the Spirit and we walk in the Spirit. However, simply using that phrase isn't enough because it's too subjective. Someone might say "the Spirit of the Lord told me," but that's an opinion which could be based upon their convictions, circumstances, or any number of things. There are people, even in religious circles, who are saying things that are untrue when measured in the light of Scripture. Even when someone holds a position of spiritual leadership, it doesn't guarantee that what they are saying is truth. There are "Christian" books and materials that don't measure up to the truth of the Bible. Unfortunately, I believe sometimes people are motivated more by the spirit of commercialism than they are by the Spirit of Truth, because there is some content that clearly does not measure up to the Word of God.

Self-Esteem

There is a significant self-esteem movement in the church world right now. It is very egocentric. It is man-centered as opposed to God-centered, and it's a deception. If we envision our life as man-centered with self as the absolute by which everything else is measured, then God is one of those influences on the periphery who, by definition, exists to satisfy us. However, Scripture clearly teaches that God is to be on the throne, not self! We must deal with self.

I once read an excerpt from a Christian book that is unscriptural and clearly consistent with the self-esteem movement. The excerpt states, "What we need in the worldwide Christian church today is nothing less than a new reformation. Where the sixteenth century Reformation returned our focus to sacred Scriptures as the only infallible rule for faith and practice, the new reformation will return our focus to the sacred right of every person to self-esteem." Another quote from the same book declares, "It is precisely at this point that classical theology has erred in its insistence that theology be God-centered, not man-centered."

I wholeheartedly disagree, because theology, by definition, must be God-centered. Anything that becomes man-centered is going to fail. Man cannot find the answer to all of his needs within himself. We are not God. We need God. The only place that we can deal with self is where Jesus dealt with it, and that is at the cross. Self has an attitude that is often inconsistent with the will of God. Jesus prayed in Gethsemane, "Not My will but Thine be done." Clearly, the two wills were not the same.

Counseling

I believe in counseling if it's biblical counseling. The Bible declares in Isaiah 9:6 that Jesus Himself is the Wonderful Counselor. Counseling is scriptural. Proverbs 19:20 states, "Hear counsel, and receive instruction, that thou mayest be wise in thy latter end." I believe in biblical counseling, but I don't believe in secular counseling. Psalm 1:1 declares, "Blessed is the man that walketh not in the counsel of the ungodly." What about Christian counseling? I want to caution you on that subject, because I fear that the phrase "Christian counseling" has at times been used as a marketing term. When I speak of counseling, I am not speaking of the experience of the counselor, but rather the philosophy and the principles of the counsel being given. The issue is not whether the counselor is a born-again Christian. The issue is the content of the counsel. Everything that is promoted as Christian counseling is not necessarily scriptural or godly. Everything must be examined in light of the Word of God.

The things which Paul wrote about in 2 Timothy 3 are coming to pass in these last days. In our society, we have so many problems, and the issue of reaching out for help and answers is becoming more and more mainstream. We must make sure we are reaching out to the right place for help, because we can open the door to ungodly things if we embrace philosophies that are not scriptural. In Chapter 3 of this book, I am going to identify ten roots of ungodly philosophy. The common denominator in this philosophy is that it puts self on the throne. We need to clearly discern these things. There is even a difference between secular humanism and religious humanism, though both are ungodly. There is a religious form of humanism, and the only way it differs from secular humanism is that it acknowledges we are created, that there is indeed a God. Secular humanism is more atheistic. Nevertheless, the philosophies that are projected in religious humanism are as deadly and as dangerous, but they are clothed in such a way that one might accept them simply because they are wrapped in a religious context.

An Unpopular Sermon

Matthew 16:21 declares, "From that time forth began Jesus to shew unto his disciples, how that he must go unto Jerusalem, and suffer many things of the elders and chief priests and scribes, and be killed, and be raised again the third day."

I'm relatively certain that the disciples disliked that sermon, because they had a totally different concept in their minds. The mother of James and John had already approached Jesus, since the disciples had the idea that Jesus was going to set up a physical kingdom on earth. They must have been thinking, "We are going to overthrow the Romans, and we are going to rule and reign. I want to reserve my seat of honor." Jesus began to teach them a truth that ran counter to this idea. He said, "I am going to Jerusalem and I am going to die, and I will be raised again the third day." They got so caught up with the "die" part of the message that they didn't hear the "raised again" part. They got upset with the thought of Jesus dying because He was their hope. They had already contemplated how they were going to be recognized and promoted and how things were going to turn out, but now their leader was saying He was going to die. Scripture goes on to say, "Peter took Him and began to rebuke Him."

I wonder if sometimes, in our own attitudes and reactions to the Lord, we do the same kind of thing. We might say, "Lord, I know your Word says that, but it just can't be right. I am not going to receive that, because it doesn't fit with my idea or desire." Peter began to rebuff Jesus and effectively said, "Lord, be it far from Thee. No. This shall not be unto Thee. This is not right. This can't be. We won't accept this." Then Jesus turned and said unto Peter, "Get behind Me, Satan." Something Peter was saying was not of God. Not long before this conversation, Peter had said something that was very much of God. In fact, it had come directly from the throne (Matthew 16:16-17). Paraphrasing Jesus' response, He said, "You didn't get that revelation from flesh and blood. You received it directly from My Father which is in heaven." Peter's divine revelation was, "Thou art Jesus the Christ, the Son of the Living God." Clearly, it is possible to have a thought, conviction, or revelation that is straight from God and then, a short time later, say something out of a spirit that still has self on the throne.

Jesus rebuked Peter by saying, "Thou art an offence unto me for thou savourest not the things that be of God, but those that be of man." Jesus didn't say the things that Peter said were things "of Satan" or "of demons." He said they were "of man." Jesus was saying, "Peter, your thinking, philosophy, conviction, attitude, and concepts are from men, from the Adamic nature. What you are saying now does not line up with the will of the Father."

Take Up Your Cross

Jesus then shared a teaching with all of His disciples that addressed the very pit into which Peter had fallen. Matthew 16:24-26 declares, "Then said Jesus unto his disciples, If any man will come after me, let him deny himself, and take up his cross, and follow me. For whosoever will save his life shall lose it: and whosoever will lose his life for my sake shall find it. For what is a man profited, if he shall gain the whole world, and lose his own soul? or what shall a man give in exchange for his soul?"

Jesus said, "If any man." Note that "any" includes all of us. He declared, "If any man will come after Me, let him deny himself." The word "deny" in the Greek means "to disown or abstain from utterly." The word "himself" is an expression of self. Jesus was saying, "Let him deny self." He then said, "…and take up his cross." Jesus didn't say "My cross." We don't carry His cross; we carry ours. Every follower must "take up his cross and follow [Jesus]," making clear that the condition of following is denial. That is, "If you are going to go everywhere that I have purposed and determined for you to go, then you must deal with self, because self doesn't want to go everywhere and do everything that I want done." You must deal with self. How do you deal with self? You deny it. You say, "Self, you will not be on the throne of my life. You are not my king."

This part of us that the Bible calls "self" is also referred to as the flesh, the old man, or the Adamic nature. This part of us says things, does things, wants things, and demands things that are inconsistent with the Father's will. Self-promoting philosophy tends to recognize self as having greater authority and power, and tends to say to us, "Obey self. Self is king. Exalt self." However, Jesus says, "Deny self. Put self in its place."

An Ugly Monster

I am not proposing some kind of self-annihilation or self-degradation. I am addressing the attitude, philosophy, and spirit within the Adamic nature that wants to run our lives. Sometimes self will literally throw a fit to get its way. It will even do things such as lying, cheating, or stealing. Self is an ugly monster. The Amplified Bible paraphrases Matthew 16:24 this way: "Then said Jesus to His disciples, If anyone desires to be My disciple, let him deny himself (disregard, lose sight of, and forget himself and his own interests) and take up his cross and follow Me (cleave steadfastly to Me, conform wholly to My example in living and, if need be, in dying also)."

Selfishness is sin. The enemy attempted to turn Christ toward self in the final hours of His life. While Jesus was on the cross, the people shouted at Him saying, "He saved others, but He can't save Himself. They in effect said, "Go ahead, Jesus, save yourself. If you be the Christ, show us. Save self" (Matthew 27:40). If Jesus would have saved self, He could never have saved us.

Jesus' "self" had to die in order for us to live. The demonic strategy was to try to "get to" that part of Him that would respond to a challenge of self. Satan had tried it at the beginning of Jesus' ministry when, in the wilderness, Satan came to Jesus and said things like, "You could command these stones to be turned to bread. You can cast yourself off this mountain, and the angels will carry you up" (Luke 4:1-13). Self can be difficult to contain when it's challenged. In fact, self manifests the most when it's challenged. For example, if somebody says to you, "You are a liar." Self says to your fists, "Tighten up." Self says to your teeth, "Grit." Self says to your arm, "Swing." Self wants to say, "Don't call me that name." We must deal with self. We are Christians. I have heard people say that "We are made in the image of God; therefore reach inside yourself. You have it all in there. God put it all there. Pull it out, put it on the throne, and it will satisfy and fulfill you." Don't believe that. It's a lie.

In Whose Image?

In Genesis 1:26, God declared, "Let us make man in our image, after *our* likeness." He made Adam and Eve in His image and likeness, but they eventually sinned. When sin entered the picture, the human race became contaminated. The nature with which you and I are born is not the pure, holy nature of God. It's the Adamic nature, the nature of sin. Genesis 5:1 declares, "This is the book of the generations of Adam. In the day that God created man, in the likeness of God made he him." When God created man, He made him in

God's image. "Male and female created he them; and blessed them, and called their name Adam, in the day when they were created."

Genesis 5:3 tells us more of the story, "And Adam lived 130 years and begat a son *in his own* likeness." Adam did not beget a son in the likeness of God. Adam's likeness now consisted of a contaminated nature, a sin nature. Every person since that time, except for Jesus, has been born in sin. The hardest thing for self-righteous people to believe is that they are sinners, because "king self" says, "You are so much better than that person who does not go to church every Sunday. You live better. You act better. And if you do everything the very best you can, you will please God." That's what "king self" says. Unfortunately, it is a lie. Isaiah 64:6 states, "We are all as an unclean thing, and all our righteousnesses are as filthy rags; and we do fade as a leaf; and our iniquities, like the wind, have taken us away." We are born in trespasses and sin. It is important that we acknowledge that truth. We must know and understand that we all have to deal with self.

The danger in ungodly counsel and philosophy is that it is egocentric. It is man-centered with everything revolving around "self." When Adam sinned, he effectively removed God from the center or throne of his life and took that spot for himself. Everything became relative to him instead of God. Like a great puzzle of life, he began assessing other people and things in his life based on how they related to him and his feelings instead of how they related to God and His Truth. We have inherited this focus from our forefathers. Self looks to man, exalts man, deifies man, and clearly omits God. Biblical counseling places God in the center and requires that every other part of our being line up with God and His Word. When Jesus came, He was revealed as the absolute, the Way and the Truth (John 14:6) and the only thing important is how we relate to Him. He becomes our focus, the center, our standard, our truth, our point of reference. Putting God in the center is the only way that brings fulfillment to man. We will never be fulfilled unless we are filled with Him. You can take self and blow it up like a balloon. You can keep pumping air into it with some kind of egotism, and it will continue to expand, but it will never fulfill you. People that have achieved the heights of popularity, fame, and fortune often testify to the fact that it never satisfies. It never fulfills. Satisfaction and fulfillment do not come out of self. True satisfaction and fulfillment come only from God.

Chapter 2

The Origin

I often say that if you can't receive the first four words of the Bible, you will have great difficulty receiving the rest of the Bible. The Bible's opening phrase in Genesis 1:1 is very important: "In the beginning God." John opens his gospel (John 1:1), similarly by writing, "In the beginning was the Word, and the Word was with God, and the Word was God. The same was in the beginning with God. All things were made by him; and without him was not anything made that was made. In him was life; and the life was the light of men. And the light shineth in darkness; and the darkness comprehended it not" (John 1:1-5). In the beginning there was only God! God was the first self. He was not a created self. He was, and is, an eternally existing self.

The Attributes of God

God, as a self, has attributes. We can categorize or classify His attributes. Some of them are called "essential" attributes. These include *omnipotence*, which means "all-powerful"; *omniscience*, which means "all-knowing"; and *omnipresence*, which means "everywhere present." He is also *immutable*, meaning He never changes, and He is *eternal*, meaning there is no beginning and no end to Him. These are essential attributes of God. There is another category called the "moral" attributes of God. The moral attributes of God include the following. He is *righteous*, He is *holy*, He is *just*, He is *merciful*, He is *love*, and He is *full of grace*.

It is important to categorize these because His moral attributes are communicable, but His essential attributes are not communicable. If God were to communicate His essential attributes, it would, in effect, mean that He is making other gods. No one is all-powerful but God Himself. No one is present everywhere but God. No one is all-knowing but God. None is immutable but God. None is eternal but God. These are essential attributes, and they belong only to God.

God existed before time ever began. Time was not made for God; it was made for man. There is going to come a point when there will be no more time. God never changes. God was full of love in the beginning, as He is now, and absolutely selfless. In His selflessness, He created angels and man. There is a distinct difference between the Creator and the created since God can communicate His moral attributes to created beings, but not His essential attributes. None of His created beings can become omnipresent or omniscient. However, His creation is so designed that they become complete only as they understand their dependence upon Him, and as His moral attributes become a part of them. John 3:16 says, "God so loved the world that He gave." I marvel at the selflessness in that! Who made God give? Who made God love? Who required of God that He be merciful? Who would have punished God if He did not have grace? He is totally selfless. He created angelic beings and human beings, and He gave them His moral attributes.

Genesis 1:26 declares, "God said, Let us make man in our image, after our likeness." Verse 27 states that He did exactly that. "God created man in His own image, in the image of God created He him, male and female created He them." He is the divine self, who is absolutely selfless. He is absolute love. He is self-giving, and He created beings that are dependent upon Him. We are not, and can never be, completely independent of God. He chooses, out of His own will and good pleasure, to create. It is absolutely impossible to prove in the Word of God that there is any such thing as evolution. God is the Creator. Creation means to make something out of nothing. God started with nothing and made something, and His creation became a dependent self. We can never be whole without Him. We are totally dependent upon Him.

Lucifer's Story

At some point after God created the angels, there was a chaotic event in heaven. Isaiah 14:12-14 tells us of this event, which is the origin of the "independent self cult," if I may use that description. Theologically, this passage is interpretable using the "law of double reference." In other words, the writer is "speaking" to one person, but speaking to them as he is speaking to a second person, similar to the way Jesus turned to Peter and said, "Get thee behind Me, Satan." Isaiah chapter 14, beginning with verse 12, states, "How art thou fallen from heaven, O Lucifer, son of the morning! How art thou cut down to the ground, which didst weaken the nations!" In this passage, Lucifer declared five things:
1) I will ascend into heaven
2) I will exalt my throne above the stars of God
3) I will sit also upon the mount of the congregation, in the sides of the north
4) I will ascend above the heights of the clouds
5) I will be like the most High

This is the seed of satanic philosophy, and it is still evident today. It is centered on the phrase "I will." That is the exaltation of self. The five things that Lucifer said all started with those two words, "I will." That is self-will. There is no mention of God's will. Lucifer said, "I will exalt *my* throne." That is self-enthronement. Then he said, "I will sit upon the mount." That is self-exaltation. "I will ascend above the clouds." That is self-ascension. "I will be like the Most High." That is self-deification. Lucifer set up a rival kingdom and a rival throne. Out of his self-will, he sought to exalt himself to the level of the One who created him.

More of Lucifer's story can be found in Ezekiel 28:11-19. Because of his "self" problem, we know that he was cast out of heaven (Revelation 12:9). There is only room for one throne and one kingdom there. However, in the satanic philosophy of self, Lucifer began something in competition with the Creator. Lucifer, an angelic being, intended to exalt himself like the Most High, and the effect of his actions eventually found its way from the angelic realm into the human realm.

Genesis 3:1 declares, "The serpent was more subtil than any beast of the field which the Lord God had made. And he said unto the woman, Yea, hath God said, Ye shall not eat of every tree of the garden? And the woman said unto the serpent, We may eat of the fruit of the trees of the garden: but of the fruit of the tree which is in the midst of the garden, God hath said, Ye shall not eat of it, neither shall ye touch it, lest ye die. And the serpent said unto the woman, Ye shall not surely die: For God doth know that in the day ye eat thereof, then your eyes shall be opened, and ye shall be as gods." There is a striking similarity between Genesis 3:5, which states, "Ye shall be as gods," and Isaiah 14:14, which declares, "I will be like the most High." The serpent told Eve, "You will know good and evil." He was appealing to her sense of self. He was appealing first to self-deification, "You will be as gods," and then to self-exaltation, "You will know good and evil."

The story continues, "And when the woman saw that the tree was good for food, and that it was pleasant to the eyes, and a tree to be desired to make one wise, and she took of the fruit thereof, and did eat, and gave also unto her husband with her; and he did eat." Adam and Eve subsequently lost the glory that surrounded them, and the shame of their nakedness became apparent. They lost the intimate relationship they had with God because they acted out of independence rather than dependence, believing the lie that something within themselves could make them complete and whole. They believed a whole pack of lies such as: "You can be as gods without God. You can know good and evil without God. You do not need God. You can be egocentric. Even though you are only a created one and not the Creator, you can take of what is in you, satisfy yourself and become whole." The basic lie was that man could be what God intended for him to be, without God. All kinds of evil things come out of independence. The enemy convinced these human beings that there was life, happiness, success, and fulfillment apart from the Creator. Lucifer knew it was a lie because he himself had fallen. A third of the angels, perhaps, fell with him (Revelation 12:9). Lucifer came to earth and injected that poisonous egocentric philosophy into humanity. "You can do it. There is nothing impossible. You can do it. Just think right. Just think positive. You can do it. You don't need God." Lies! Lucifer stepped out of created order. He stepped out of God's beautiful plan and design, and in a spirit of independence, set up his own throne and put his own king, self, on the throne.

Genesis chapter 5 tells us the result, and this is why every one of us who are sons of Adam are born with the "self" problem. Genesis 5:3 declares, "And Adam lived 130 years, and begat a son in his own likeness, after *his* image." The same Hebrew words for "image" and "likeness" are used in Genesis 1:26-27 and Genesis 5:3. Every person born since the fall was made in Adam's image and likeness, born in sin. We are born sinners, and there is no way we can spin that differently or dress it up. There is some theology that says we are born in the image and the likeness of God, so we have God in us when we are born. In truth, we have sin in us when we are born, and self is on the throne, because we are created in the image and likeness of Adam. Adam had fallen and had become independent of God, and he became selfish, self-centered, egocentric, and egotheistic. Here is the truth: there is no hope for man outside of God. Being born-again, being reconciled to God through Jesus Christ, is not a religion. It's not a theology. It's not a philosophy. It's the only way to deal with the fact that we have been independent; we have been alienated from God. We are born alienated. *We are not sinners because we sin. We sin because we are sinners.* Out of the nature comes the act, so we have to deal with the nature as well as the act.

Humanism

Humanism preaches that man is autonomous. By definition, that means that man can exist by what is within himself, and he has the right to govern himself. It means that he can be completely independent of God. However, Scripture teaches otherwise. Man is not autonomous. Man is dependent on God. Without God, we will never have eternal life. Without God, we will never know love. Without God, we will never have grace or mercy. The moral attributes of God can only be communicated to us as we receive Him. Otherwise, we are morally bankrupt. The philosophy and psychology that is being communicated today teaches that there exists within man, as a human being, all that is necessary to govern himself, fulfill himself, and make himself happy and whole.

We stare into the face of all of the statistics, the mounting crime, the degradation in society, and yet we still perpetuate the lie. Lucifer did the same thing. He had fallen, and he still sold the lie. Humanism essentially says, "God? What do you mean God? We don't need God. What is this about God?"

There are some basic ideas that secular humanism sets forth. Secular humanism is most often atheistic, which teaches there is no God. Other strains of humanism are agnostic, which takes the position of saying, "We are not certain whether there is a God or not." Humanism preaches evolution. According to humanistic philosophy, man is not a created being. He is an animal that evolved and is still evolving. Humanism preaches that man is autonomous, that he is the center and the sum of all things. It says that man is capable of existing independently of God, and he has the right of self-government. Humanism says that man is the measure of all things, that he is able to meet his own needs, and that he has the answer to all problems within himself. Humanism says that man is not really a sinful being in need of salvation, and in fact, man is his own god. He is egotheistic. Humanism is entirely man-centered. It says that all the human needs can be met in man, for man, and by man. The subtle problem is that there is a religious form of humanism. Religious humanism acknowledges that there is a God, but the subtle error is that it still contends that man is autonomous, that man can meet all his needs by drawing on what is already inside of him. It teaches that your behavior is a function of your environment, so if you fix the environment, it follows that you will behave rightly.

This philosophy is being taught in colleges and universities, high schools, and even grade schools. It's being taught to our children. The emphasis on self-esteem is taking hold in the lives of many people. It teaches that the problem with you is that you don't think highly enough of yourself, but in truth, the only place we can deal with self is at the cross. Self-will never satisfies. If you pursue happiness, you will never be fulfilled. If you pursue pleasure, you will never be fulfilled. If you pursue your own advancement or recognition, you will never be fulfilled. If you climb the ladder, you will find that there is nothing to be found there. If you chase the rainbow, you will find out there's no satisfaction. Man, independent of God, cannot be fulfilled. If you try to pump yourself up, like putting air in a tire, the only thing that may happen is you will eventually deflate or explode. You won't be fulfilled. The real answers are still in the Bible.

Reconciled to God

I am not promoting self-annihilation or self-flagellation, or recommending the physical torture of the flesh. However, we must deal with this ugly thing called "self" that wants its way and demands the throne of our lives. "Self" demands to be pleased and satisfied, honored and obeyed, and it attempts to convince us that, if we dedicate our lives to that end, we will be whole, happy, and complete. It's a hollow, empty lie. Satan pursued it to his detriment, then he planted that ugly lie in the mind of man. The beautiful thing about the work of Jesus Christ is not just that He forgives us our sins through His blood, which is glorious, and not only that He convicts us and convinces us that we are sinners by His Holy Spirit, which is beautiful, but, the miracle of miracles is that He can reconcile us to God. We can be brought back on friendly terms with God. We can love God and be loved by God. We can commune with God and fellowship with God. We can be living epistles, known and read of all men (2 Corinthians 3:2-3). People can see Jesus, rather than self, in us. We became the mess we are long before we were born into this world. I think it's important to know where this self thing started. It wasn't that way in the beginning, and praise God, it's not going to be that way in the end.

The Word of God

Let's not be drawn into the unbiblical web of those who teach things that sound good or seem to make sense at the moment. The Word of God is all that will last, though heaven and earth pass away. The Word of God stands from the beginning and through eternity without any need for altering, upgrading, modifying, or modernizing. The Word of God is forever true. Syncretism, meaning a mixture of truth and untruth, is so apparent in the world today. I don't speak against ministries or against people, but please hear me when I say that not everything you pick up in a Bible bookstore is full of biblical truth.

Likewise, every teaching CD or DVD that is produced is not scriptural. We can't just swallow something because we see a scripture reference in it, and we think, "This must be true; it has scripture in it." Many times, scriptures are quoted out of context and their meaning is distorted. We must know the whole Word of God. We must not isolate scripture or "proof text." We must not come with a preformed opinion and then try to gather scriptural bullets to substantiate that opinion. We must take the whole Bible from Genesis to Revelation, and let God reveal Himself through it. God is at work. The only way He can really be glorified through us, and we can be used for His purpose, is if we deal with "self." We can all identify with this struggle. At some point in time, in each of us, self-will has manifested through self-ambition, self-enthronement, self-exaltation, selfishness, or many other "self-ways." The only way we will ever become selfless is as the Spirit of Christ dwells in and works through us. Even in church, self can manifest itself. "That is mine, and don't you dare touch it." "Brother, you are in my pew." "I can't stand that worship song." "I just don't like the book of Jeremiah. Lead me to the Psalms." I believe that as we recognize the ugly monster of self, and we don't try to pet, justify, or protect it, and we call it what it is - *sin* - then God can forgive us and heal us and our society.

I pray that God will grant us fresh revelation and understanding, until this ugly thing that has come through the Adamic nature will appear so undesirable to us that we will cry out for self to be taken off the throne. Jesus said in Matthew 11:28-30, "Come unto me, all ye that labour and are heavy laden, and I will give you rest. Take my yoke upon you, and learn of me…For my yoke is easy, and my burden is light."

Chapter 3

The Mixture

In 2 Corinthians chapter 11, Paul was writing to a group of people in whom he had personally invested much teaching and mentoring, helping them to grow in the things of God. The church at Corinth was in the midst of a city full of idolatry and darkness, but there was a group of believers there that had tapped into the things of the Spirit. They had grown in God, and they had learned much about the deeper things of God. However, Paul, in this particular passage, expresses a concern that I believe the Holy Spirit carefully recorded, because it continues to be a concern of our Lord toward all of us. Paul writes these words in 2 Corinthians 11:3-4, "I fear, lest by any means, as the serpent beguiled Eve through his subtilty, so your minds should be corrupted from the simplicity that is in Christ. For if he that cometh preacheth another Jesus, whom we have not preached, or if ye receive another spirit, which ye have not received, or another gospel, which ye have not accepted, ye might well bear with him." In verse 3, Paul was expressing a very important concern to the believers in Corinth. He did not want them to be beguiled (deceived) by the serpent as Eve had been deceived in Eden.

The intention and the desire of the serpent is that our minds, understanding, and thoughts would be corrupted, tainted, diluted, confused, and distracted from the simplicity that is in Christ. God wants us to have a singleness of mind and a pure devotion to Christ. Another translation says: "But I am afraid lest, as the serpent deceived Eve by his craftiness, your minds should be led astray from the simplicity and the purity of devotion to Christ." Paul was communicating the desire of our Lord that we not complicate or contaminate our pure and simple devotion to Christ.

Syncretism

I believe that Paul expressed this concern because Satan's intention is to dilute our relationship with Christ. Syncretism is defined as "mixture." It is the combining and the uniting of things or peoples that are unlike. Applying it spiritually, syncretism is the mixture of the purity of the Word of God and the psychology that exists in the world today. Psychology by definition is "the behavior patterns in the mind; the thought patterns of our lives." There is an attempt on the part of the evil one to take the humanistic philosophy of the world and mix it with the purity of the Word of God. His goal in doing so is to deceive or beguile us, such that we fall away from the simplicity and purity that should exist in our relationship to the Lord. Much of the "garbage" that has been packed into our heads over the years proves to be a hindrance that threatens to complicate and contaminate what is intended to be simple and pure.

Many times, the enemy tries to complicate, confuse, and contaminate by using religious words and phrases. We can find this in materials in Bible bookstores, as well as teaching CDs and DVDs. The word "spiritual" is used over and over, and "spiritual" can be interpreted as synonymous with "scriptural" if we don't carefully understand what is being said. Many of these "spiritual" movements attempt to draw people into a pattern of thinking or a lifestyle that has a connotation of being religious but, in fact, is absolutely unscriptural and unbiblical in every way. The deceit of that is to draw us away from the simplicity and purity of our devotion to Christ. If we lose pure devotion, we have lost everything. As a result of many of these philosophies and teachings, people have actually contrived another Jesus. They have created, in their minds and conversation, a Jesus that isn't in the Bible, a spirit that isn't the Holy Spirit, and a gospel (good news) that isn't the Gospel of Jesus Christ. It is false, it is ungodly, and it is wrong.

Don't Be Deceived

Satan is so clever that he will even quote portions of Scripture like he did when he tempted Jesus on the mountain (Luke 4:1-13). We must not be misled simply because we see a scripture reference in the middle of an article. That doesn't mean that the article is biblical or scriptural. It may be inserted there to deceive. We must read, understand, and use discernment. Paul the Apostle was saying, "My Christian brothers and sisters who I birthed in the Lord and taught the ways of the Spirit, please know that this danger threatens to overtake and overcome you."

I believe God is saying to the church today that it's very important for us to sort these things out. We must know the Word of God and the ways of God. We cannot embrace everything we hear or see on the internet, radio, television, CDs, or DVDs. Anyone who has a voice can record a CD, and anyone who has a pen can write a book, but that doesn't make them true. Unfortunately, there are a lot of sincere people that are taken in. One of my intentions is that we will more clearly identify some of these things so we do not fall victim to deception.

The children of Israel got into trouble on their journey in the wilderness because of the mixed multitude. There were people who didn't believe in Jehovah "mixed" in with the believers. The mixed multitude created an appetite and lust for the things of the flesh. In the books of Exodus and Numbers, it was the mixed multitude that influenced the children of Israel away from the purity and the simplicity of the things of God, and they ended up desiring the things of the flesh. It is that mixture that is most dangerous. Most of us love the Lord enough that if the enemy appeared before us and said, "I am Satan. I have something to say to you," we would say, "Get behind me. Get out of here. I don't want to hear from you. You have nothing to say that will do me any good"

However, the enemy doesn't approach us that way. He comes in a "spiritual" book. He comes on a "religious" CD. He puts on his religious garment, but if you look at it very closely, it's not pure. It's not clean. It's contaminated with humanism, New Age philosophy, and egotism. It is egocentric – centered around man as the absolute, not God. Anything egocentric is eccentric. That is, anything that is centered on man is off center. The Bible teaches that only Christ-centric or theocentric is correct. That is the secret of life. Jesus effectively said, "If you are going to follow Me, the first thing you have to do is deal with self." You must deny yourself (Matthew 16:24).

The Deception

We must examine Genesis chapter 3 to see exactly how "the serpent deceived Eve." Genesis 3:1-6 states, "Now the serpent was more subtil than any beast of the field which the Lord God had made. And he said unto the woman, Yea, hath God said, Ye shall not eat of every tree of the garden? And the woman said unto the serpent, We may eat of the fruit of the trees of the garden: But of the fruit of the tree which is in the midst of the garden, God hath said, Ye shall not eat of it, neither shall ye touch it, lest ye die. And the serpent said unto the woman, Ye shall not surely die: For God doth know that in the day ye eat thereof, then your eyes shall be opened, and ye shall be as gods, knowing good and evil. And when the woman saw that the tree was good for food, and that it was pleasant to the eyes, and a tree to be desired to make one wise, she took of the fruit thereof, and did eat, and gave also unto her husband with her; and he did eat."

Genesis 3:4 declares, "And the serpent said unto the woman, Ye shall not surely die." Of course, he was lying! Verse 5 states, "For God doth know that in the day you eat thereof, then your eyes shall be opened, and ye shall be as gods, knowing good and evil." He was referring to the fruit of the tree which was in the midst of the garden, which was called the Tree of the Knowledge of Good and Evil. Please note the mixture in that name "good and evil." *God said to eat of the Tree of Life, and Satan said to eat of the mixture.* It wasn't called the "tree of the knowledge of evil." It wasn't called the "tree of evil." It was called the Tree of the Knowledge of Good *and* Evil. It is a mixture. The serpent said, "God knows that when you eat of that tree, your eyes are going to be opened and you are going to be as gods, knowing good and evil." What a lie!

Verse 6 declares, "And when the woman saw that the tree was good for food, and that it was pleasant to the eyes, and a tree to be desired to make one wise, she took of the fruit thereof, and did eat." What appealed to her? The *good* and the *pleasant*. What did she desire? Wisdom. She saw that it was good, it was pleasant, and it offered wisdom. "She took of the fruit thereof, and did eat, and gave unto her husband with her, and he did eat." She wasn't intentionally seeking something evil. Yes, she was disobeying God, but the serpent offered her something that looked good, pleasant, and was desirable to make one wise. It was inviting to her, and it didn't appear blatantly "evil."

We may wonder, "How could she be so deceived?" We must understand that Satan was appealing to that which looked good and pleasant to her. She was attracted by it, but it was a mixture. God said, "Stay away from the mixture. I have a tree over here that is pure. I have a tree (the Tree of Life) that is uncontaminated, and there is no confusion. There is simplicity and purity in this tree." That tree represents Jesus, the living Word. However, there is another tree that Satan is going to try to make look appealing to us. He will appeal to our intellect and curiosity in order to deceive us. We may even look at the thing that God said not to touch and think, "There is a part of this that really looks good and pleasant. This would be wise for me to do." Sometimes, there is apparent wisdom even in ungodly philosophy, but God didn't say that the problem was that it was unwise. He said it would bring *death*. He was saying, "If you eat, swallow, and ingest it, and make it a part of you, it will bring death, but what I have for you will bring life." Eve succumbed and accepted the contaminated mixture. "She took of the fruit thereof, and she did eat, and gave also unto her husband with her; and he did eat. And the eyes of them both were opened, and they knew that they were naked." We know the rest of this tragic story. Unfortunately, it didn't end on that day. We are all products of what happened in the garden.

New Age philosophy is a contaminated mixture. If we swallow it, it will bring spiritual death. It will make us self-centered. In that mindset, if something ceases to serve self, we reject it – and that includes God. Unfortunately, over the last number of years, I feel that there has been some extreme preaching that has almost presented God as existing only to serve us and make us happy. People that have swallowed this teaching and haven't heard the entirety of God's truth have, in many cases, eventually become disappointed and disillusioned. In some cases, they have turned away from God and walked their own way. Jesus said, "If you want to follow Me, you must deny yourself." He said that the first thing we must do is change from being egocentric to being Christ-centric (or theocentric, which means God-centered). The first thing we must do is put the correct Person in the center. If we do not place God in the center, we are "missing the mark," which is the very definition of the term "sin." Sin can only be dealt with at the cross. The church must get back to the message of the cross and the blood. That is the message of life.

Jesus taught that the fruit of the tree originates from the root of the tree. He said if the root is good, then the fruit will be good; and conversely, if the root is bad, the fruit will be bad. We can identify what the tree is like by looking at the fruit, but the source of that fruit is the root.

I would like to examine what I believe to be the root of this ungodly fruit of humanism and New Age philosophy that is presenting itself as a mixture. It is just like the tree in Eden, a tree of mixture that has some glamour, glitter, and pleasant appeal. It looks good, and it suggests that we will be a lot wiser if we pursue it, but the source of all goodness and wisdom is found only in Jesus.

We will briefly examine ten philosophies or movements based on falsehoods that I believe have contributed most significantly to bringing this mixture to the world. In the same way that God instructed Adam and Eve not to touch the fruit of the "mixture tree," we must stay away from "mixture thinking," because these are the roots of the bad fruit. Humanistic New Age philosophy came from these roots, and this philosophy has been gradually expanded upon over the years. This is not an exhaustive list, but I believe this will help us to be aware so we will not be victims of the mixture (syncretism). We will not be deceived like Eve was, and therefore we will not reach out for something that may appeal to our desires, appetites, or emotions, as opposed to the purity of the Word of God.

The Lie: Economic Equality is the Answer

This philosophy teaches that man is essentially an animal, a materialistic creature, and his deepest needs can be met by economic equality. In other words, if he has all he wants in terms of materialism, he will be whole, happy, satisfied, fulfilled, and complete. Over the decades, the errors of this philosophy have been exposed on a global scale through the failures of communism, but millions of people have bought into this thinking. Jesus said in Luke 12:15 that "Man's life consisteth not in the abundance of the things which he possesseth." He was saying that we can grasp, obtain, and attain material things, but they will not bring fulfillment and wholeness to our soul or spirit. I am not declaring that there is anything wrong with material things. I am referring to the appetite, the insatiable hunger that is materialism, like when we think to ourselves that if I can only obtain this or that, I will be happy. For example, "If I could only get that job..." or "Oh, if I could just have that car..." There is nothing wrong with a good job or a nice car. However, this philosophy teaches that if everything is equally divided, and everyone has all they need and want, people will be happy. What a lie. There is certainly a glitter to material wealth. It looks good and pleasant, but the deception is its mixture, and it still leaves people empty. I remember sitting across the desk from one of the vice presidents of a corporation who, with tears running down his cheeks, said to me, "I thought this was what it was all about. I worked, sacrificed, and did everything possible to achieve success, but somewhere along the road I lost my home, marriage, and family. I have lost everything that is really important to me. I am very unhappy. This isn't where it's at."

The Lie: Man's Deepest Need is Pleasure

This philosophy states that man's deepest need is pleasure and most of man's problems stem from his past. This philosophy essentially says, "You were hurt by your parents, your friends, your family, or your church. You have been victimized. You have been suppressed. You have been dealt with wrongly."

It is true that many people have been treated wrongly, and have had very bad experiences. Unfortunate things have happened to them. But again, the answer to that is at Calvary, finding healing in Jesus. We can't forever blame our condition on the way we were treated. We need to take our issues to the cross, receive healing, and get on with walking with Jesus.

The answer to fulfillment and wholeness is not in pleasure. Hebrews 11:24-26 states that Moses, because he had respect unto the recompense of the reward, chose to "suffer affliction with the people of God, [rather] than to enjoy the pleasures of sin for a season." The Bible acknowledges that sin can be pleasurable, but this pleasure is clearly temporary. It only lasts "for a season." Sin sometimes looks good to the eye, but the truth is found in Psalm 16:11, "In thy presence is fulness of joy; and at thy right hand there are pleasures for evermore." God's presence brings true and lasting pleasure. *Forevermore* is much better than *for a season!*

Why choose the mixture? Why choose the fruit that looks appealing but will not satisfy? Why choose the fruit that brings death? Have you ever made the mistake of biting into a piece of wax fruit, thinking it was real? It didn't satisfy. In fact, if you eat too much wax fruit, it could bring death. It sure looks good. It's beautifully shaped and colored. It looks like you could peel that orange. How many people are attracted by the pleasure of sin for a season but do not see the beauty, glory, and the forevermore pleasure that is in God's presence? The only way we can truly convince someone is to lead them into His presence. Once people really know what it's like in His presence, it's much more difficult for the enemy to make that "syncretism tree" look so good.

The Lie: Man is a Product of His Environment

This philosophy teaches that man behaves like an animal, and, as a result, he is not responsible for his behavior. It teaches that man's behavior can be manipulated and governed by environmental conditions, and in effect, if we make the environment right, then man will behave right. It is not true, but it is an appealing political message. Candidates stand on a political platform and say, "Elect me and I am going to fix things up, and when I'm done changing the environment, we are not going to have crime anymore." I am convinced that until man's heart is changed, we will have crime, regardless of the environment. I appreciate and love a beautiful environment, but it cannot change the heart and behavior of man. Isaiah 64:6 declares, "We are all as an unclean thing, and all our righteousnesses are as filthy rags;

and we all do fade as a leaf; and our iniquities, like the wind, have taken us away." There is something wrong inside of all human beings. The fallen nature, the Adamic nature, is wrong. Humanism says, "Change the environment and behavior will change." Jesus says that is not true. Jesus wants us to take that ungodly behavior to Calvary and crucify it, call it sin, and repent of it. We must draw upon God to make the changes necessary in our life, and then *we* will change the environment! We are called to be the light of the world and the salt of the earth (Matthew 5:13-14). We are called to affect others around us. Sometimes we blame our condition or circumstances on others, but doing so prevents us from being healed and getting changed. As long as we can blame someone else, we don't have to deal with ourselves. We sometimes blame our parents and grandparents for the way we are. In Jesus, every generational curse is broken. We don't have to be like anyone that went before us. Generational curses can be broken.

The Lie: Man Needs Power

This philosophy acknowledges that man is a human being, not an animal. It teaches that inside man is a lust for power, dominion, and control. Therefore, the evil of man's life results from the fact that he isn't able to get the power he wants in order to meet his needs. If man had the power he needed, he could meet all of his own needs. Please note the account of Simon the sorcerer in Acts 8:14-25. Simon was a well-known man who had power, control, and authority. Then he became a believer in Jesus. One day he saw Peter and John laying hands on people, and the people were receiving the Holy Ghost. Simon said to them, "I want that kind of power. I have never had that kind of power. May I purchase that power from you?" Simon had come to Jesus, but he hadn't dealt with his appetite for power. In effect, Peter said to him, "Your money be cursed with you. This kind of power can't be bought with money. You must repent because I see a gall of bitterness and bond of iniquity in you. There is something that has been carried over from the past, and you are going to have to deal with that. I will tell you how to deal with it, Simon. Repent. Put your money away and repent." Throughout history, many leaders have risen to prominence with an insatiable lust for power. Often times, terrible tragedies have resulted because this power was in the hands of men who had self on the throne of their life.

The Lie: Knowing the Meaning of Life is the Most Important Thing

One philosophy declares that man's greatest problem is that he needs to know the meaning of life. He needs to know what life is all about, and when he understands that, then all of his needs will be met. However, the Bible tells us what life is really all about. James 4:14 says that it appears as a vapor for a season and then it vanishes away. It is there, and it is gone. The thing that is meaningful, and which changes us, is not understanding human life, but *receiving* divine life, which is everlasting (John 3:16) and abundant (John 10:10). God doesn't say we need to understand more about human life. He effectively says, "If you will come to Me and acknowledge that you have come short of My glory, if you come to Me and acknowledge that it's only through Christ you can know life, then I will give you life." True life isn't something we can attain by learning or applying our ingenuity. It's something we receive by faith in Jesus Christ.

The Lie: The Problem is Wrong Behavior toward Our Fellow Man

This philosophy states that man's problems stem from bad behavior, *not* wrong behavior toward God, but rather wrong behavior toward his fellow man. This is one philosophy that has a religious garment on it, and therefore, deceives many people. It teaches that all we have to do is get our human relationships straightened out. We don't really need God. We just have to get together in something called "integrity groups." We get together, open up to each other, and tell everyone about our problems. We tell them how bad we are, what we really feel, and what we really think, and if we do enough of that and we get this horizontal communication going, then we will be OK. This philosophy is becoming popular, but Jesus made the truth very clear when He said, "Without me, ye can do nothing" (John 15:5). We cannot become fulfilled by improving our horizontal relationships. We will not meet our needs by pouring out our problems to everyone else and letting them pour out theirs to us. That will not make us whole. God wants us to open up to Him, and let Him come into our life.

The Word of God does say in James 5:16, "Confess your faults one to another," and followers of this philosophy can quote that scripture to make their way of thinking somewhat appetizing. Notice that James wrote, "Confess your *faults* one to another," not, "Confess your *sins* one to another." We are to confess our sins to God. He is the only one that can deal with sin. We can confess sin to one another and it may relieve some guilt because we have spoken it, but it doesn't remit the sin. Only the blood of Jesus remits sin. Humanistic philosophy has been woven into the thinking of many people, and different types of "group therapy" have become increasingly popular. There is nothing wrong in coming together in groups, as long as God is invited and remains the focus, but the root of this ungodly philosophy is wrong.

The Lie: Man is Basically Good

This philosophy teaches that man is basically good and there is such a thing as evil, but it's not within the individual; it's within society. Proponents believe if you change society, you will change the individual. This is basic humanistic, man-centered thinking, and it contends that if we look down deep enough inside, we will find that we are really good. Sometimes we say, "There is good in everyone," and that is true to some extent, but way down inside, we are all sinful. We are like an apple that is rotten at the core. In fact, Psalm 51:5 declares that man is born in sin and shapen in iniquity. We can't simply blame society for everything and say, "If we can get society straightened up, life is going to be wonderful, because we are all good people." That is nonsense. Before we come to Jesus, we are full of pride and arrogance and rebellion. But the "man is basically good" philosophy is presented in such a soft light. They say, "Look for the good in someone. Then change society around them and you will see their 'good' blossom as a rose, and it will be wonderful." Not true! The only place that a rose blooms is at the foot of the tree at Calvary. We are all born in sin and shapen in iniquity.

The Lie: Man is Self-Sufficient

This teaching declares that man is autonomous, which means "self-sufficient." It advocates that man has everything within himself that he needs. He doesn't need anyone or anything, no external influence, nothing at all. It says that we don't need God. God just gets in our way. We have all of the resources needed to do everything that we will ever want to do. We have all we need to find fulfillment, joy, happiness, wholeness, and healing. We have it all inside; all we have to do is access it. However, that is the sin of the garden - independence. The serpent essentially said to Eve, "You shall be as gods. You will be able to function independently now. You will know good from evil. You won't need God. You are autonomous. You will get to a level where you can satisfy yourself." Paul put it this way in Colossians 2:10, "Ye are complete in him." We become whole and complete only in God. We cannot become complete in ourselves. We are fragmented and incomplete. We are not whole. We do not have within us the resources which are necessary to save ourselves, make ourselves well, reconcile ourselves to God, or remit our own sin. We do not have the resources necessary to justify or redeem ourselves. All of that comes only from God.

The Lie: Believe in Yourself, and You Can Do Anything

Another philosophy is called self-actualization, which really is the quintessential egocentric philosophy. It says that, if you believe in yourself enough, you can do anything that you aspire to do. It says that, if you have enough faith in yourself, you can achieve it, experience it, live it, and know it - just believe in yourself. That's a lie. The Word of God makes it very clear in Acts 16:31, "Believe on the Lord Jesus Christ, and thou shalt be saved." The word "saved" means "the whole provision of God for the whole man, everything you need from God for your spirit, soul, and body." We can psyche ourselves up and believe in ourselves more and more, but there is no scriptural basis to say that there exists, within fallen man, the strength through the power of belief to do the things that can only be done through Jesus Christ.

The Lie: Man's Greatest Need is for Self-Esteem

This movement teaches that man was made in the image of God and therefore, man's greatest need is for self-worth, self-esteem, and self-love. It says that the need for dignity, self-worth, self-respect, and self-esteem is the deepest of all human needs. However, this pursuit of self-esteem and self-actualization has a very real danger of introducing pride and arrogance into the soul of man. The Word of God (James 4:6, 1 Peter 5:5) tells us that "God resisteth the proud, but giveth grace unto the humble." The pursuit of self-esteem is very popular in our day, and it takes a lot of different shapes and forms. Possibility thinking is one of them which says that if you have the right kind of mental discipline, ordered thoughts, and conviction in your soul, it will bring about the very thing you are dreaming or speaking about. It's another very humanistic form of setting God aside and saying God is not the greatest need of man. It says that elevating man to a point of appreciating himself and believing in himself will meet his deepest needs. The subtle danger is its implication that we can actually become something out of our own power and strength, whether it's mental, psychological, or some other expression. It implies that we can become something outside of Christ, outside of God.

The Truth: Our Sufficiency is in Christ!

Some of these humanistic philosophies contain a smattering of truth, and that's exactly why they are so deceptive and dangerous. While some humanists, and those that promote godless philosophies, deny the existence of God, very few do. Most acknowledge that there is a God, and most believe that man is a human being, not an animal. However, they are directing us to look into ourselves, elevate ourselves, enlarge ourselves, and put ourselves on the throne, and in doing so, we are somehow going to find fulfillment and satisfaction. However, while they are going through this entire exercise, they have taken God out of the picture. They allow for the fact He exists, and they may even admit that He created the universe, but they do not acknowledge that we are absolutely dependent upon Him for every breath, every decision, everything. The egocentric spirit of independence is loose in the world today, and it is clothed in religious garments so that we will eat the fruit of that tree because it looks good. The truth is that we need Jesus, and Jesus will bring what we need! I am not saying that He will not help our self-esteem, but He will not do it by elevating our "self" in place of Him. We will be strengthened because of His presence within us. He is our righteousness, our holiness, and our justification. He is everything. It is Him, in us, that makes us complete. "Ye are complete in Him" (Colossians 2:10). It's Christ in us that is the hope of glory (Colossians 1:27). I cannot take Him and put Him aside and run my own life. It won't work. I will end up empty.

John MacArthur, in his book *Our Sufficiency in Christ* writes, "Psychology cannot really study the soul; it is limited to studying human behavior. There is certainly value in that, but a clear distinction must be made between the contribution behavioral studies make to the educational, industrial, and physical needs of a society and their ability to meet the spiritual needs of people. Outside the Word [of God] and the Spirit [of God], there are no solutions to any of the problems of the human soul. Only God knows the soul, and only God can change it. Yet the widely accepted ideas of modern psychology are theories originally developed by atheists on the assumption that there is no God and the individual alone has the power to change himself into a better person through certain techniques."

We need God, not materialism. We need God, not an improved environment. We need God, not pleasure. We need God, not power. Anything that does not revolve around Jesus Christ, around God, is eccentric. It's off center. When we put man in the middle, and put self on the throne, we are off center. It won't work. It won't change the soul. We might be able to change, to an extent, man's outward behavior, but we can't change the inner man except by the power of God, the blood of Jesus, the name of Jesus, and the cross of Calvary. We need to deny self. We need to crucify self. We need to put self where the Bible says it belongs - on the cross, not on the throne of our lives. That is the way to wholeness in life.

Chapter 4

Counseling

"Counseling" is a word that we hear frequently today. It seems that if we have a question that may, for the moment, defy an answer, someone will say, "Get some counseling." It is becoming very popular. We will examine counseling from a biblical standpoint as well as from a humanistic, psychological standpoint. We will pray that the Lord will help us to be able to receive that which is truth and be able to discern that which is not, enabling us to lay it aside.

Wonderful Counselor

Counseling is biblical. Isaiah 9:6 prophesies about the coming of Christ, "Unto us a child is born, and unto us a son is given" and refers to Jesus as Wonderful Counselor, the Mighty God, the Everlasting Father, and the Prince of Peace.

Jesus has given gifts to the church, according to Ephesians 4:8-13. He bestowed gifts when He ascended on high. He gave them to the church for the purpose of the perfecting of the saints, the equipping of the saints, and the building up and edifying of the body of Christ. One of those gifts is counseling. Proverbs 11:14 tells us "in the multitude of counselors there is safety." It is clear that this gift of counseling is given by our Lord Jesus Christ to His body, His people, so that we may benefit thereby.

Biblical Counseling

Biblical counseling is scriptural, proper, and accepted by God. A New Testament word that is used frequently in the King James Version is the word "admonish" or "admonition." This word has the same meaning as the word "counseling." The Greek word is *noutheteo*. In another form, it means "to gently correct, to warn, to give guidance, to give understanding, and mild rebuke." The initial definition is "to put in mind" these kinds of things. So whenever the New Testament uses the word "admonition" from the Greek word *noutheteo*, it includes mild rebuke, correction, warning, and direction. The scriptural purpose of counseling is not simply confirmation but also correction. Correction is something that is usually abrasive to our human nature. The one being counseled usually likes confirmation. If the counselor doesn't give confirmation, the person may try a number of other counselors until he receives confirmation, when the counselor tells him what he wants to hear. We need to understand that biblical admonition isn't simply confirmation. It is often correction, and we all need correction from time to time.

Sometimes, we need to be gently prodded and warned. The word "gently" is a part of the definition of *noutheteo*. God doesn't want counselors to come down on people in a forceful, judgmental, condemning, and commanding way. Instead, He wants the counselor to be like a shepherd who leads his sheep to direct them, correct their path, and use his staff to gently bring them back into line. We seem to be people who easily get out of line and find ourselves going astray. God's provision for us includes correction, and He tells us that correction can come from many sources. By looking at some places in the New Testament where that Greek word *noutheteo* is used, we can get an understanding of what God means when He says that we need to be admonished.

Romans 15:14 states that believers are to "admonish one another." We are to minister to one another, so it follows that we are to receive ministry from one another. That doesn't mean that we receive direction from everyone that speaks. First Thessalonians 5:12 declares, "Know them which labour among you." However, we must be open to the fact that God can give us a word through others. First Thessalonians 5:12 and Titus 3:10 both teach that leaders are to admonish believers. Sometimes we don't like leaders to say things to us that involve warning, correction, or gentle prodding. We all tend to like things that excite us and make us feel good. However, if we are going to grow, become strong and be rooted (planted, firm, stable, and consistent) we need admonishment. Leaders are responsible under God to give that gentle guidance, correction, and encouragement.

Colossians 3:16 declares that one of the ways believers admonish one another is through psalms, hymns, and spiritual songs. First Corinthians 10:11 states that the experiences of Israel are written for our admonition. In other words, God recorded all of these things so that we could be cautioned, gently reproved, admonished, warned, and mildly rebuked. Ephesians 6:4 says that fathers are to bring up their children in the nurture and admonition of the Lord. There are times that a father must give gentle reproof and mild rebuke and, on occasion, strong rebuke. It comes with the responsibility of being a father. We all need to be corrected and directed sometimes, and God gives us spiritual fathers and natural fathers for that purpose.

The Greek word *noutheteo* is also used in Acts 20:31, 1 Corinthians 4:14, Colossians 1:28, and 1 Thessalonians 5:14.

Paul the Apostle ministered in various churches and counseled them as a spiritual father. In the book of Acts, and in his letters to the Corinthians, Colossians, and Thessalonians, Paul ministered to the churches with what we call "nouthetic counsel." He counseled them with mild rebuke, correction, and gentle prodding. There are times when we are to edify and there are times when we are to admonish. All edification and no admonishment produces spoiled children. All admonishment and no edification produces bondage. We need to both *direct* and *correct* in love, and all of these elements are a part of it. They are all a part of God's plan and provision.

We counseled people in the local church that I pastored for many years. We preferred to use the term "personal ministry." We selected that term for several important reasons. First of all, it is intended to be ministry, spiritual enlightening, and spiritual blessing to those that receive. We did not pretend to be professional counselors in the sense of having achieved certain degreed academic learning. However, we felt the responsibility to biblically admonish, encourage, strengthen, and lift up. We therefore embraced this ministry that was first in Christ Jesus and then, by the Holy Spirit, in the New Testament church. I believe it's an important part of the spiritual growth and development of many people. We embrace this as a ministry, being careful to understand that it can only be effectively carried out through the person of the Holy Spirit, and we therefore always seek the anointing of the Holy Spirit.

Worldly Counseling

Let's look at what the world usually calls "counseling," which I believe can more accurately be defined as "humanistic, psychological reasoning." In Isaiah 30:1-3, God is giving rebuke to His people Israel. Isaiah writes, "Woe to the rebellious children, saith the Lord, that take counsel, but not of me." It is clear that there is a kind of counsel that is not of God. Isaiah wrote that they "cover with a covering, but not of my spirit, that they may add sin to sin." In their rebellion, they cover the sin of rebellion rather than dealing with the sin. Therefore, they add sin to sin, which is devastating. We cannot remove sin without dealing with it. Covering sin will not remit it. Covering sin accumulates it, which is in effect simply adding sin to sin. People can get caught in this vicious cycle. They do something wrong, then they lie about it to cover it up. If someone challenges the lie, they lie about the lie. Then things snowball, and they lie about the lie about the lie. It starts getting thick, but underneath it all, the sin is still there. In Isaiah chapter 30, God was speaking to Israel and saying, "There is rebellion in your heart and in your spirit."

God had a rebellion problem with Israel, but the difficulty was not just the fact that they were rebellious. The difficulty was that they, through the wrong kind of counsel, were covering the rebellion rather than identifying it and dealing with it. God essentially said that they were layering their sin by adding sin on top of sin, and the pile was getting high. In other words, wrong counsel can complicate a situation and cause further harm. Wrong counsel isn't merely useless; it is actually destructive. It isn't as if good counseling will help and wrong counseling does nothing. Wrong counseling will actually destroy.

What kind of counsel were the people of Israel getting? In Isaiah 30, God told them, "You walk to go down into Egypt." I have that word "down" circled in my Bible because I see it not only as a geographic pointer, but I see it as a spiritual thermometer. When we head toward Egypt, we are on our way down. Egypt is symbolic of everything that brings bondage, sin, and confusion. In Isaiah's time, Egypt was monotheistic in religion. Their religion centered on one god, but that god was the sun. Their kings were called "pharaohs," and they had an elaborate system of idolatry in the sphinxes and the pyramids, which were the tombs. Egypt was a very powerful force in that day. Egypt had the most highly regarded university in the entire world, the "University of Egypt." That's where Moses received his academic education. God was effectively saying there was an Egypt mentality, an Egypt psychology, an Egypt counsel that existed. It had a very loud voice, and the people of Israel were tuned into that voice rather than the voice of God. They were listening to this Egypt kind of thinking. God was saying, "You have gone down to Egypt, and you have not asked what I have to say about situations. You have not sought My word. You have not sought My direction. You have gone down into Egypt, and you have drawn from what Egypt says and how Egypt thinks with the intent of strengthening yourself in the strength of the Pharaoh, and you have put your trust in the shadow of Egypt." God felt violated. God was the one with the sure Word, the only Word that works, the only solution to the problem, and the only answer to the question, but they were not asking God what He thought. They chose instead to hear what Egypt said and how Egypt thought.

As New Testament believers, we can make the mistake of listening to what "Egypt" has to say without seeking God. It's not that we conclude God doesn't have the answer. However, sometimes in our busyness, we are actually being shaped by, and subscribing to, the mentality of Egypt simply by not seeking the face of the Lord. God basically said, "I have wisdom; I have a word; I have provided a way of life for you, Israel. If you will only seek Me and reach out to Me, I will give it to you." We need to continually seek the Lord.

Perhaps one of the most dangerous things that can happen to us is to rest on our laurels. We learn a few things, then we relax. We need to tune into God every morning. We need to acknowledge our need for His direction, guidance, wisdom, mercy, grace, love, protection, care, and correction every day. We don't even have to ask for it from the world for it to infiltrate our thinking. If we simply turn on the computer or television, or pick up the newspaper, it's there. Egypt is confronting us continually. If we do not discern that fact and deliberately seek God, we can find ourselves victimized. All of a sudden we can begin to think like, talk like, and act like Egypt and we wonder, "How did that happen? I never decided to become an Egyptian." Egypt is all around us.

God was saying something important to Israel in Isaiah 30:3: "Here is what happens; here is the consequence of not asking at My mouth, of not seeking Me and not getting good counsel, of covering your sin with a covering and not dealing with it. Therefore shall the strength of Pharaoh be your shame." In other words, even if you get what you are seeking, you won't be happy with it. You will be ashamed of it. Even if you attain and obtain, it will not satisfy or fulfill. God was saying, "Your trust in the shadow of Egypt is going to end up bringing confusion, not help, to you."

The counsel of the ungodly will confuse, because the ungodly are confused. I sometimes wonder if it's a waste of time to listen to the media. There seems to be a lot of perversion, "spinning," and subtle, hidden motives. It sometimes seems that instead of simply reporting the news, they are interpreting the news and telling us how we should think about the news. If we are not careful and discerning, we can start thinking the way they are thinking. This is a serious problem. Ungodly counsel is not of God, and it covers sin rather than dealing with sin.

Biblical vs. Worldly Counseling

How can we distinguish between humanistic, psychological counseling and biblical counseling? I would like to suggest six measures to determine whether counsel we receive is of God or not. If it doesn't pass these six tests, we should not listen to it or embrace it. We need not only to be aware of the spiritual experience of those whom we are listening to, but we also need to be aware of their own philosophical convictions, because that is the base from which they counsel. This word "Christian," I am afraid, has been sorely misused to the profit of some. Someone figured out the fact that if they put a shingle over their door calling themselves Christian, it will attract a certain clientele that they wouldn't otherwise reach. We must be careful not to conclude, that just because someone calls himself a Christian, he is counseling biblically. I am saddened to report this.

Some people use the word "Christian" to basically mean "non-heathen" or "non-pagan." We like to think it means "biblical, scriptural, and godly." I think that is what it should mean. A number of years ago, during the Charismatic movement, I used to hear the phrase "Spirit-filled" all the time, to the point that it was overused. What exactly do they mean by "Spirit-filled"? Does it mean at some point they received the baptism of the Holy Spirit? Does it mean they speak in tongues? Does it mean they smile and dance?

I believe there are good biblical tests that can be helpful as we decide what to listen to and receive in our lives. When I speak of counseling, I am not just speaking of sitting across a desk from someone, because the word "admonition" in the Bible is used for preaching and teaching as well. Humanistic psychology is actually being preached in some pulpits today, and we must take measures to avoid it.

Six Questions to Ask Your Counselor

These are six questions you can ask your counselor to determine whether they are likely to give godly counsel. You need to ask about their philosophy and their theology, because those things determine the methods they use and the advice that they give.

1) *Are they an atheist or an agnostic*? You might be surprised by how many atheists and agnostics can use terms that sound spiritual. Atheists say there is no God. Agnostics say they aren't certain if God exists. Ask: "Are you a born-again believer?" If they aren't, don't go to them for counseling.

2) *Are they an evolutionist or a creationist?* This will indicate the counselor's attitude toward Scripture.

3) *What is their attitude about the Bible*? Do they believe the Bible is the Word of God and that all Scripture is given by inspiration of God? Do they believe the Word of God is inerrant? If the person you are listening to does not absolutely believe that the Bible is the Word of God – that every scripture is divinely inspired and inerrant - then all of their counseling and philosophy is going to be on the wrong base. "As [a man] thinketh in his heart, so is he" (Proverbs 23:7). Find out what they believe.

4) *Do they believe in the fall of man*? This is important because out of that comes the knowledge that the nature of man is sinful. Man is born in trespasses and sin and,

therefore, needs redemption. He doesn't need covering; he needs remission of sin. He needs repentance. There is no other way to be free from sin. The blood of Jesus and the name of Jesus are the precise areas that will quickly separate the humanists, because they keep looking for redemption inside of human beings. However, the truth is that deep down inside is sin and iniquity, and a need for Jesus. It doesn't matter how intelligent, beautiful, or talented a person may be. We are all born dead in trespasses and sin.

5) *What do they know about the redemptive truths as they are revealed in Christ?* What do they know about redemption, repentance, faith, justification, and sanctification? How does man come out of spiritual death into spiritual life? What is the process? Is it just being mentally persuaded, or is there a need for a supernatural work of God, a Holy Spirit miracle to take place, a new birth, a regeneration of our spirit? Our spirit is dead and must be resurrected. This is very critical. These things are foundational truths and principles of the faith.

6) *How do they propose to deal with man's problems and needs?* Do they deal with it out of secular humanistic philosophy, the self-help movement, by discovering oneself, or by seeking God by the power of the Holy Spirit to reveal the things of God to us? We are born into this world very egocentric. In our fallen nature, we feel that we are the center of life and everything revolves around us. The fallen nature embraces the things that are comfortable to the "I", the "me," the "self." The tragedy is that we reject the only way of salvation. The convicting work of the Holy Spirit is essential to change. When God gets through to us, He changes us to be Christ-centered. We come to understand that we are to serve Him, not vice versa. We begin to understand what life is all about. *Me* is not where it's at. *He* is where it's at. The more we look to Him, the more we are changed from glory to glory into His image (2 Corinthians 3:18). John the Baptist in John

3:30 said, "I must decrease, and He must increase." He was essentially saying, "I am dealing with two things. I am dealing with *I* and I am dealing with *He*. I start out with the big *I* and the little *he*, and that is my problem. But as I become whole, the big *I* becomes the little *i* and the little *he* becomes the big *He*. Then life takes on fulfillment and meaning and purpose.

The Place of Blessing

In Psalm 1, God speaks of the place of blessing. Where is the place of blessing? He starts with the negatives. He said we are blessed if we *don't* do these things. "Blessed is the man that walketh *not* in the counsel of the ungodly." This is not limited to counsel from ungodly people; it includes unscriptural counsel even from godly people. Even people that know the Lord can potentially give ungodly counsel.

The man is blessed because he makes a decision, "I am not going to walk in the counsel of the ungodly. I refuse to walk in the counsel of Egypt, and I refuse to sit in the seat of the scornful." Continuing on, Psalm 1 states, "Nor standeth in the way of sinners." Notice all three attitudes there, represented in all three postures: walking, standing, and sitting. It presents a picture of regression.

We've covered the negatives: "Blessed is the man that doesn't…" Let's now look at the positives. Blessed is the man whose "delight is in the law of the Lord; and in his law doth he meditate day and night." Notice that it doesn't say that the blessed man meditates on God's Word once a week. It says "day and night." The word "meditate" doesn't necessarily mean that we are consciously thinking of it all the time. Life demands us to be consciously thinking of other things. Psalm 1 is referring to the workings of the heart and the spirit, where the Word of God is going over and over inside of us all the time. That is often happening even when we don't realize it. Some people burst out spontaneously with an "Amen" because the Word is turning over inside them, and when they hear something which witnesses with their spirit, they automatically say "Amen." There is something going on inside, and it cannot be contained.

Psalm 1 continues, "And in his law doth he meditate day and night. And he shall be like a tree planted by the rivers of water." The blessed man is planted. His roots are down. Believers have a privilege that unbelievers and the ungodly don't have. They don't know the Truth. They haven't seen the Light. They don't know anything but darkness. Their existence only consists of the things of this world. We are not simply blessed because we know there is another way. We are blessed because we walk in that way. A person that knows to do good and doesn't do it is missing the mark.

Chapter 5

An Important Triad

In this chapter, we will address three things that relate directly to the kingdom of self. They are: the curse, the cause, and the cure. We can think of the curse as the problem, the cause as the reason for that problem, and the cure as the solution to that problem. There is a problem, a reason, and a solution; the curse, the cause, and the cure.

Let me use a common illustration. Suppose you have a fever, and you go to the doctor, who examines you and says, "You have a fever." Would you be happy if that's all he did? No, because you can put a thermometer in your mouth to determine if you have a fever. The issue is not that you have a fever; the issue is why you have a fever. You want to know the cause of the "curse," the cause of the problem. Once the doctor knows what is causing the fever, he can work on the cure. He doesn't just seek to cure the fever; he seeks to cure the cause of the fever. A fever, though we tend to see it as an affliction, is really a blessing. God built that into the human body. A fever is a "red flag" which indicates there is something wrong in the body that needs attention. Don't just curse the fever; rather, curse the cause. The fever goes away when the cause is cured.

The Curse

Let's look at this in the context of "the kingdom of self." Humanity is living under a curse which originated in the Garden of Eden. Genesis 3:14 states, "The Lord God said unto the serpent, Because thou hast done this, thou art cursed above all cattle, and above every beast of the field; upon thy belly shalt thou go, and dust shalt thou eat all the days of thy life: And I will put enmity between thee and the woman, and between thy seed and her seed; it shall bruise thy head, and thou shalt bruise his heel. Unto the woman he said, I will greatly multiply thy sorrow and thy conception; in sorrow thou shalt bring forth children; and thy desire shall be to thy husband, and he shall rule over thee." That was a curse.

The Bible account continues, "And unto Adam he said, Because thou hast hearkened unto the voice of thy wife and hast eaten of the tree, of which I commanded thee, saying, Thou shalt not eat of it: cursed is the ground for thy sake; in sorrow shalt thou eat of it all the days of thy life. Thorns also and thistles shall it bring forth to thee; and thou shalt eat the herb of the field; In the sweat of thy face shalt thou eat bread, till thou return unto the ground; for out of it wast thou taken: For dust thou art, and unto dust shalt thou return." That was a curse.

Adam and Eve's son, Cain, killed his brother Abel, and Genesis 4:9 speaks of the consequences, "The Lord said unto Cain, Where is Abel thy brother? And he said, I know not: Am I my brother's keeper? And he said, What hast thou done? the voice of thy brother's blood crieth unto me from the ground. And now art thou cursed from the earth, which hath opened her mouth to receive thy brother's blood from thy hand; When thou tillest the ground, it shall not henceforth yield unto thee her strength; a fugitive and a vagabond [a wanderer] shalt thou be in the earth." That was a curse.

"Cain said unto the Lord, My punishment is greater than I can bear" (Genesis 4:13). Because he killed his brother, Cain was cursed to be a wanderer for the rest of his life in the earth. There is a powerful lesson here, that if we don't deal rightly with our brother, we may end up wandering spiritually. There are a lot of people wandering all over the church world today because they haven't made certain things right with people. They have become spiritual wanderers. They never are planted, settled, or rooted. They are always wandering because there is an issue that was never dealt with. In the natural, this was so with Cain, and there was a curse that came. Later in the book of Genesis, God said that He would curse anyone that cursed Abraham. God repeated that to Isaac and to Jacob. He said to the children of Israel, "If you don't obey My word, curses will come upon you. If you do obey, blessings will come your way." (See Deuteronomy 28:1-68.) Throughout the Scriptures, again and again, there is evidence that a curse has come upon humankind.

In Matthew 24, Jesus said that the evidence of this curse would be particularly apparent in the end times. He said that there would be wars, rumors of wars, pestilences, plagues, earthquakes, famines, national conflicts, and economic disasters. We can easily see the curse in action in humankind through suicides, drug and alcohol abuse, immorality, homosexuality, adultery, fornication, incest, bestiality, murder, divorce, child abuse, rape, satanism, occult religions, mental illness, hatred, violence, social disorder, anarchy, and euthanasia. It's amazing what this ugly, humanistic, ungodly spirit is doing. Mankind has already participated in killing the young via abortion. Now society is attempting to devalue the elderly via euthanasia, as well as cutting off other people that we think are no longer able to make a contribution to society. All the while, scientists are experimenting with genes in the laboratory to try to make a perfect man. The problem is they can't even define "perfect." It is clear that we are living in a world that is cursed.

Everyone admits that we have serious problems in our society which are out of control. We do not have the answer. There is no argument when it comes to the acknowledgement of the fact that there is a "curse," a problem, which exists. At the point of defining the cause, a difference of opinion arises. Because there is disagreement about the cause of the curse, it follows that there is disagreement about what the cure is. Everyone, even the ungodly, admits we have problems - murder, drug addiction, immorality, and suicide, to name a few. You do not have to be spiritual or biblically sound to acknowledge that there is a problem. However, once the curse is acknowledged, then we have to be careful to acknowledge the cause.

The Cause

Proverbs 26:2 declares, "As the bird by wandering, as the swallow by flying, so the curse causeless shall not come." That is sixteenth century King James English, and it's kind of hard to understand that last phrase, so allow me to state it in twentieth-first century English. God says here, in His Word, that the curse shall not come without a cause. Where there is a curse, there is a cause. "The curse causeless shall not come." Another way of saying it is, we will always find there is a cause for the curse. That is a principle in Scripture.

Secular humanists say that the cause for the curse lies in the matter of self-esteem. They say the cause is that we either have too much or too little self-esteem. They say the reason that the number of murders are increasing is because we have a self-esteem problem; the reason for all of society's ailments lies with the lack of self-esteem. One book on self-esteem states, "There are many studies today which document the scientific fact that a lack of self-esteem is at the root of alcoholism, teenage rebellion, marriage and family breakups, and all sorts and varieties of crime." In other words, the need for self-worth and self-esteem is the greatest of all human needs in the world today. Without proper self-esteem, it is impossible to solve the world's problems. Proponents of secular and religious humanism attribute the cause of these serious issues to a lack of proper self-esteem. Therefore, people are asked to take positive steps to enhance their self-esteem. In other words, they are saying the lack of self-esteem is the great sin of the human race. If you can solve that, you will solve all of these other problems.

But what does the Bible say? Psalm 51:5 declares, "Behold, I was shapen in iniquity, and in sin did my mother conceive me." That is *not* saying that we were conceived immorally. It is saying that, at the time of our conception, the nature of sin was a part of us. So what is the cause? The cause, the Bible teaches, is neither the lack of self-esteem, nor the overabundance of it. The Bible teaches that the cause is sin. Romans 6:23 states, "The wages of sin is death." *The wages (the curse) of sin (the cause) is death.* Sin comes first, causing the curse. We were conceived in sin, shapen in iniquity. We are born with the sin nature, and because we have the sin nature, we commit sinful actions. We are not sinners because we sin. We sin because we are sinners. The cause is the sin nature. The result of sin is death. Romans 3:23 says, "For all have sinned and come short of the glory of God."

Secular humanists and religious humanists believe that is too simplistic an answer. They say the Bible is for simple-minded people. They must complicate it, and they complicate it right out of the realm of truth. If we acknowledge that our problem is sin, then we are set to deal with the cure. However, if we embrace the lie that our problem is because we have too little self-esteem or too much self-esteem, then we have a problem with the cure. We will live our whole lives being angry at those who wronged us. Jesus said He didn't come to call the righteous; He came to call sinners to repentance (Matthew 9:13). We can never know repentance unless we acknowledge we are sinners. Basic to the work of salvation is the acknowledgement that we have sinned and come short of the glory of God. It is not just the fact that we have done things wrong, but that we are sinners by nature. Our salvation doesn't rest in our ability to list all of our failures. It rests in our ability to acknowledge that we are sinners by nature, by birth. We couldn't possibly remember everything we did to miss the mark. I'm so glad that salvation isn't based on that.

Mark 7:21-22 declares, "For from within, out of the heart of men, proceed evil thoughts, adulteries, fornications, murders, thefts, covetousness, wickedness, deceit, lasciviousness, an evil eye, blasphemy, pride, foolishness. All of these things come from within and defile the man." Galatians 5:19-21 states, "Now the works of the flesh are manifest, which are these: adultery, fornication, uncleanness, lasciviousness, idolatry, witchcraft, hatred, variance, emulations, wrath, strife, seditions, heresies, envyings, murders, drunkenness, revelings, and such like: they which do these things shall not inherit the kingdom of God." We are shapen in iniquity and conceived in sin (Psalm 51:5). Flesh, self, wants to do those things. If we let self have its way, it's going to do them. Self has appetites, ambitions, and desires that are inconsistent with the will of God. Peter spoke up and effectively said, "Jesus, that thing you just said about dying cannot be true. We will not accept that" (Matthew 16:22). I wonder how many of us would have reacted as Peter did? Peter had walked with Jesus for over three years, placing all of his hopes and ambitions in Jesus' establishment of an earthly kingdom. Many of us would have likely agreed with Peter. In the sense of morality, Peter's thought wasn't evil. He wanted to keep Jesus with him, but the Father's will was for Jesus to go to the cross and deal with sin. Yet what Peter said was sinful. Why was it sinful? Because it missed the mark. It made sense, but it was sin. We can do things that make sense and yet they are sin. We can miss the mark.

The Cure

Let us acknowledge, as the Scriptures teach, that the cause of the curse is sin. It has nothing to do with self-esteem. It has nothing to do with self-confidence or self-actualization. Therefore, if we are going to cure this curse, we must deal with the cause. If the fever is going to go away, we must do something about what is causing it, and that is exactly God's plan and God's program. In Christ is the answer. The blood of Christ will remit sin. It's the only thing that will remit sin. It is the cure.

We cannot take Jesus, the Word of God, out of the picture and have a cure, because the problem is sin. We cannot simply take the bottle away from the alcoholic and cure him. We tried that in the Prohibition era, and many men became wealthy with underground stills. The problem isn't the bottle; it's the appetite. The bottle is just the "fever." The appetite is what is causing it. We must deal with the cause. That may sound simplistic, but it's biblical. You might say, "Pastor, do you mean that this individual who is an absolute human wreck can simply come to the cross of Jesus Christ, bow his knee, acknowledge 'I am a sinner, and I receive you Jesus as my Lord, and I ask you to wash my sin in your blood, come into my life' – and that simple little act will completely cure the cause?" Yes. It's that simple. That is the gospel of Jesus

Christ. "Him that cometh to me, I will in no wise cast out" (John 6:37). Humanists try to deal with the effects of the curse without dealing with the cause. The curse has effects. You have a fever, and the effect is that you have no strength. You are in bed, and you can't get up. You don't feel well. In this case, you don't deal with the effect of the curse. You deal with the cause of the curse. If you are dealing with the effect, you are never going to cure the cause. The cure is in Christ.

Self-Esteem Propaganda

A couple once gave me a copy of a paper that was being distributed and taught in the public school system in a city near my home, and it is an example of what I am talking about. It was treated as a professional resource, and was available to the teaching staff. It quotes a song called "The Greatest Love of All" which says, "I believe the children are our future. Teach them well and let them lead the way. Everybody's searching for a hero. People need someone to look up to. I never found anyone who fulfilled my need, a lonely place to be, so I learned to depend on me. Because the greatest love of all was happening to me, I found the greatest love of all inside of me." That is clearly humanistic. The greatest love of all is not inside of us. It's in Christ Jesus. God is love. This paper went on to say, "Ultimately, we must all learn to trust ourselves and our own insights. There is no right or wrong way in the world, just a way that works for you." That is relativism. The Scriptures teach absolutes, that there is a right way, and there is a wrong way. In fact, the book of Proverbs says, "There is a way which seemeth right unto a man, but the end thereof are the ways of death" (Proverbs 14:12). There is a way that we know is wrong, there is a way that seems right, and then there is a right way. In John 14:6, Jesus said, "I am the way."

This paper had a section on affirmation. It began by quoting Proverbs 23:7 completely out of context. "As [a man] thinketh in his heart, so is he." If we read the entire context, it in no way suggests that, resident within the heart of the unconverted, ungodly human is the ability to become whatever he wants to become. "The objective here," the teachers were told, "is to empower students to overcome negative attitudes and learning blocks and to develop greater self-esteem by affirmations. And affirmations, by definition, are positive statements which declare a desired objective as if it were already achieved. The power of affirmation increases by linking it to a visual image of the desired outcome." Here is a combination of teaching them to say what they want, and by visualizing that thing in a very positive way, suggesting that it will make what was visualized come to pass.

We have to be very careful in our religious teaching, too. It is important that our teachings agree with the Word of God. It's my conviction, in the whole of the Word, that God is the initiator and we are the ones who align ourselves to believe what He has said. We don't *initiate*, we *respond*.

"And so," the paper went on, "teach the children to follow the procedure of relaxing, breathing deeply, imagining the scene, and then ask them to speak to themselves the things that they want to happen." Self-esteem is addressed. "The inner peace that emanates from a child with a positive self-image is a major component of a peacemaker. Belief in the wise part within and an awareness of their positive attributes allows children to face the world without fear, empowering them to create a positive future for themselves." Can you see the subtle hideousness of the enemy? Can you hear the serpent in the Garden of Eden saying, "Just look at that tree!

Isn't it beautiful to behold? Imagine it. See it. See what you can become. Think. Oh, forget what God said. Come out of yourself." It's the same poison.

The answer, my friends, is not in imagery. It's not in positive affirmation. It's not in trying to dig down inside to find that little bit of self-esteem and cultivate it until it is bigger. The answer is falling on our faces at the cross and saying we have sinned and come short of the glory of God. It's not what I want to be, but rather what He wills for my life, that really matters.

There is a balance to this. I am not suggesting that there isn't a right way to think. Philippians 4:8 says that we ought to think on the things that are pure and of good report and honest, and we need to discipline our thoughts. But let us not think that God has placed within us the creative power to use the thought process or the imagination to bring to pass those things that we choose.

Seven Things We Need

There are seven things we need. We need genuine repentance from dead works, repentance from sin. We need genuine faith toward God through Christ and not faith in self. We need self-denial and all that means from the biblical viewpoint. We need to accept the cross, both the cross of Christ and the Christian's cross. We need to follow Christ wholeheartedly and unconditionally. We need revelation in our heart of what it means to be in Christ. We need a revelation of Christ in us.

Our Inheritance

Let us contrast what we inherited in Adam with what we

inherit in Christ through the cross. In Adam, we inherited a self-will, an independent, autonomous spirit. In Christ, we inherit God's will and dependence on God. In Adam, self-belief; in Christ, faith in Christ. In Adam, self-love; in Christ, love for God and others. In Adam, self-deification; in Christ, self-humbling. In Adam, self-exaltation; in Christ, self-evaluation. In Adam, self-worth; in Christ, worthy is the Lamb. In Adam, self-gratification; in Christ, self-denial. In Adam, self-confidence; in Christ, confidence in Christ. In Adam, self-centeredness; in Christ, Christ-centeredness. In Adam, self-actualization; in Christ, self-control. In Adam, self-transformation; in Christ, regeneration. In Adam, self-esteem; in Christ, esteeming others higher than ourselves. In Adam, selfishness; in Christ, self*less*ness. In Adam, the kingdom of self; in Christ, the kingdom of God in Christ. We inherit in Adam the kingdom of darkness. We inherit in Christ the kingdom of Light. In Adam, we inherit problems and needs. In Christ, our problems and needs are met in Him. In Adam, a self-filled self; in Christ, a Christ-filled self.

Within us does not exist the ability to fulfill the deepest cry and the deepest longing of our life. We cannot make ourselves whole. That is an exercise in futility. Only Jesus can make us whole. I pray that God will give us such clear understanding that the philosophy of darkness will not invade our hearts but that we will have a desire to press in to Christ, draw near to Him, reach out for Him, and open ourselves to all that He says and all that He provides. He will satisfy the deepest longings of our heart. He is the only answer. There is a curse, a cause, and a cure. The cure can be found at the old rugged cross.

Chapter 6

Battle for the Throne

How do we dethrone self? How does the Bible tell us we are to overcome self to the extent that we can enjoy the victory and liberty that results? I wish that I could say it results from a single experience, but I don't find this idea in the Word of God. I believe the Scriptures teach that it comes out of a process of continually yielding ourselves to the Lord as the Holy Spirit directs and prompts us. There are occasions when we rejoice in seeing victory over some expression of self in our lives only to find down the road that God identifies another area we need to address. His purpose is to bring all of these things under control, and He deals with us line upon line, precept upon precept, here a little, there a little (Isaiah 28:13), that He might accomplish the fullness of His purpose. Every one of us is somewhere in the process.

I believe there are two particular events in Scripture that help us to understand how to deal with self. After we examine these two events, we will look into the Pauline Epistles as Paul gives us some application of this truth, so we can apply it to our lives today.

Barabbas or Jesus?

The trial of Jesus Christ is one event that can teach us how to deal with self. We will focus upon Pontius Pilate and his role in Jesus' trial. Pilate was the fifth Roman procurator of Judea, and his area of jurisdiction not only included Judea, but it also included Samaria and the area as far south as Gaza and the Dead Sea. He had a considerable geographic influence, and there were thousands of Jewish people living in his area of jurisdiction. Perhaps the most significant issue he ever dealt with was the trial of Jesus.

Beginning with Matthew 27:15, the Bible says, "Now at that feast the governor was wont to release unto the people a prisoner, whom they would." In other words, according to Jewish custom, a prisoner would be pardoned and released to the people during the Passover Feast. Pilate was in a tough spot because the crowd was pressing for the crucifixion of Jesus, yet Pilate found no fault in Him. Pilate was looking for an alternative. Verse 16 declares, "They had then a notable prisoner, called Barabbas." The Gospel of John says that Barabbas was a robber. Both Mark and Luke tell us that he was a murderer. The composite of those accounts shows us that Barabbas was a thief (he took what didn't belong to him), and he was a murderer (he took human life). His character fits with John 10:10, where Jesus says of the devil, "The thief cometh not, but for to steal, and to kill, and to destroy." Satan's desire is to rob and kill, as well as to destroy. That same spirit was in Barabbas.

The word "Barabbas" carries an interesting meaning. The prefix, *Bar,* in front of a name means "the son of; the descendant of." The second part of the word, the suffix, specifies who they are descended from. The suffix of "Barabbas" is *abbas*, from the root word *abba,* meaning "father." Therefore, by definition, the word Barabbas means "the son of a father" or "the descendent of the human race." Wherever names, places, or numbers are given in the Bible, they have very special significance. Barabbas' name identifies him as the descendant of a man, if you will, of the human race. Barabbas was noted for the fact that he was a thief and a murderer. That is the spirit of the man. He was driven by his own self-pleasure and self-exaltation, even at the expense of others and their lives.

Barabbas stood on one side of Pilate, and Jesus on the other. Verse 17 states, "Therefore, when they were gathered together, Pilate said unto them, Whom will ye that I release unto you? Barabbas or Jesus which is called Christ?" Please see this picture: On one side was the son of a man (human seed); On the other side was *the* Son of *the* living God (divine seed). This was the contrast. Pilate was in effect saying to the people, "One of these can be released to you at this season. One of these will walk among you, talk to you, walk your streets, live in your neighborhood, influence your thoughts, and touch the lives of your children. One of these will be received and will be among you and identified with you. Do you want it to be the seed of the human race, that self-serving, stealing, murdering Barabbas, or the life-giving Son of God, Jesus?"

There is a battle regarding who will sit on the throne of our lives. We only have one throne, but there are two contenders. We only have one place of lordship and authority. Jesus said in His teaching, "No man can serve two masters" (Matthew 6:24). He said we will either love the one and hate the other or cling to the one and despise the other. He said it's absolutely impossible to put opposites on the throne. They are mutually exclusive. If self is on the throne, Jesus isn't. If Jesus is on the throne, self can't be.

Pilate's Dilemma

This was the dilemma of Pilate. He brought it before the people, and they were faced with the issue. We may have supposed that the people would have immediately said, "Give us Jesus." What had Jesus done when He was among them? He had fed them, healed them, freed them, taught them, and blessed them. Jesus, in command and in control, brought blessing for three and a half years. He blessed the people. He still does. But the issue was: "Who do you want on the throne of your life?" The people wrestled with it.

The next verse declares that Pilate "knew that for envy they had delivered [Jesus]." They hadn't delivered Jesus for fault, failure, or evil, but rather for envy. "When [Pilate] was set down on the judgment seat, his wife sent unto him, saying, Have thou nothing to do with that just man: for I have suffered many things this day in a dream because of him" (Matthew 27:19). This speaks volumes to me, because I believe every time we face a decision of whether to let self rule or let Jesus rule, there is the faithful influence of the Holy Spirit saying, "Don't turn Jesus away." Self may be appealing for a season, but the worst mistake we can make is to deny Jesus. It is much better to deny self. By way of a dream given to Pilate's wife, the faithful influence of the Holy Spirit came. He comes to us in the midst of our haste to provoke us to consider the implications, consequences, and importance of the decision. We are what we are because of choice. We must stop calling ourselves victims and blaming everything on someone else. There are some people that never take responsibility because they say that it's always someone else's fault. We must stand up as men and women of God and make a choice. If we don't choose Jesus, self will automatically occupy the throne. The consequence of that is destructive. Through self, the enemy tries to steal from you what God wants you to have, and, if he can, he tries to kill you. Barabbas is the thief and the murderer. Those are his credentials and he manifests those things through *self*.

If you are a born-again believer, you came to Jesus Christ and you acknowledged that you had sinned and come short of the glory of God. You said, "Jesus, I want you to forgive my sins and come into my life." In doing so, you chose the redemptive work of Jesus Christ over your own self-righteousness. You said, "I have sinned." Self doesn't like to admit that, but it is the only way you can be saved. Jesus can't save anyone but sinners. You must say, "I have sinned. I am a sinner." You can't just say, "Adam sinned." You can't get saved for Adam, and he can't get saved for you.

Like Pilate, we have to make a decision. We have a choice to make, either to pursue the son of flesh (Barabbas), or the Son of God (Jesus Christ). Unfortunately, the pressure was so great that Pilate gave in to it. He didn't hear the prompting of the Holy Spirit, and he yielded to the pressure. No matter who your neighbors, co-workers, or classmates may be, no matter what the pressure is around you, don't compromise Jesus. Don't be ashamed of Jesus, and don't be ashamed to tell anyone, "I choose Jesus." Whether they are pleased or not, whether they will be your friend or not, whatever it costs you, don't back down simply because the flesh says, "I want to be accepted. I want to be highly regarded. I want to be honored. I want to be popular." Take that flesh and move it off the throne and say, "I want Jesus," because that is the way of true life.

The Battle in the Garden

Pilate wasn't the only one that dealt with the battle between the kingdom of self versus the kingdom of God. Even Jesus had to deal with self. Matthew chapter 26, beginning in verse 36, declares, "Then cometh Jesus with them unto a place called Gethsemane." The word "Gethsemane" means "the place of the oil press." That was the place where the olives were pressed and the olive oil was taken. Oil is a type of the Holy Spirit and His anointing. There is spiritual symbolism here in this passage. I firmly believe that the degree to which we walk and function in the anointing is a consequence of the extent to which we have dealt with self. It's in the place of the oil press where the issue is faced. It was there that Jesus entered into the battle of "self versus His Father." Who was going to be on the throne? You and I are Christians today because He won that battle.

Jesus won the battle, and He won it in the place of the oil press. Words are inadequate to describe it, because I have always believed that Calvary was carrying out what had been settled in Gethsemane. Jesus walked it out on Calvary to fulfill the Word of God, but He fought it in Gethsemane. Jesus the Son of God was sinless. He had the Spirit without measure. God the Father was well pleased with Him. Yet, even Jesus had to deal with self.

Sometimes we think we are so spiritual that we don't have to deal with self. That is not true. That is deceptive. The enemy is a liar. To walk out Father's purpose for His life, Jesus had to do something that the flesh didn't want to do. We all have had times when we had to force the flesh to do something it didn't want to do in order to fulfill God's purpose for that moment. Our flesh does not always want to pray, read the Word, go to church, witness to the lost, or love our neighbor.

Matthew 26:36-38 states, "Then cometh Jesus with them unto a place called Gethsemane, and saith unto the disciples, Sit ye here while I go and pray yonder. And he took with him Peter and the two sons of Zebedee, and began to be sorrowful and very heavy. Then saith he unto them, My soul is exceeding sorrowful, even unto death." Please see the press that was upon Him. The press was so heavy that it felt like death. "Tarry ye here and watch with me." Jesus knew where to fight the battle. He knew how to deal with the conflict. He went to the place of prayer. "And he went a little further, and he fell on his face, and he prayed, saying, O my Father, if it be possible, let this cup pass from me: nevertheless not as I will, but as thou wilt." Jesus' own self-will was for the cup of suffering to pass from Him. That is what He willed or He would have never said, "Nevertheless, not My will." However, He in effect said, "Father, that is My will, but I submit My will to Your will. There is only one throne here, Father, and I want My will to be dethroned and Your will to be enthroned if Your will is different than My will."

The account in Gethsemane only takes a few seconds to read, but I believe it took hours to live, and the intensity of that struggle is recorded not only by Matthew but by other Gospel writers. Jesus goes on after He finds His disciples asleep, and effectively says in verse 41, "Pray that you don't enter into temptation." The Living Bible paraphrases that as, "Keep alert and pray. Otherwise temptation will overpower you." Here is the principle. Jesus revealed it as He said, "The spirit indeed is willing, but the flesh is weak." You have to deal with both spirit and flesh. Jesus prayed again, "Father, if this cup may not pass away from me except I drink it, thy will be done." Verse 44 declares that He prayed a third time, saying the same words. Jesus knew what He would face, and that is why He was talking about the weakness of flesh and the willingness of spirit. He knew that the conflict was for occupation of the throne. It was the kingdom of self versus the kingdom of God.

It may have taken several hours, but Jesus settled it. Later that night, the soldiers came, led by Judas, to arrest Him. Jesus wasn't angry at Judas. He didn't fight the soldiers. Why? Because the battle was already over. The issue had already been faced. It was settled. Jesus told Peter to put away his sword. "You don't understand, Peter. Self is still on your throne. But it's not going to be for long, Peter, because the Holy Spirit is going to deal with self in you, too, when you realize that what you thought was your bold affirmation for Me turned out to be nothing more than a whim. But, Peter, when you find out that you are not everything you thought you were, don't be discouraged, because I am going to be right there to lift you up. I am going to be right there to help you take that old self, Simon, off the throne and put the new man, Peter, on the throne."

We have all had to battle self, and perhaps we have all occasionally lost the battle. Jesus prayed all night. He was in emotional agony. The tremendous stress caused Him to sweat a mixture of perspiration and blood (Luke 22:44). Dealing with self is not a superficial issue. Self is so deeply engrained and rooted in us that we do not even know the stronghold it has until we face something, and self rears its head and says, "I will not give in. What do you mean forgive? I am not going to forgive. They did me wrong. I didn't receive the respect I was due. I didn't receive the honor. I didn't receive the acknowledgement. I didn't receive the visibility." Self is ugly.

I believe that the extent to which we are effective and fruitful is a consequence of this issue. I am not talking about whether we are going to heaven or not. If we are born again, we are going to heaven. That is settled.

Natural, Carnal, Spiritual

The church at Corinth, though it was in the middle of one of the most ungodly cities in New Testament days, was a relatively spiritual church. Most of the teachings that we have on spiritual gifts and spiritual fruit come from Paul's letters to the church at Corinth. However, in their midst, there was also a great deal of carnality. Let me define the three terms that Paul used. He spoke of the "natural man," the "carnal man," and the "spiritual man." By brief definition, the *natural* man is the one that is not regenerated, not born again, not saved. That is the way we are when we are born in sin. The *carnal* man is the one whose spirit is alive. He is regenerated, he is born again, but self is still on the throne. The *spiritual* man is the one who has dethroned self and enthroned God. The teachings of Paul show us that you can be spiritual at one point and carnal at another point, then spiritual again and then carnal. It isn't as if once we have a moment of spirituality, carnality is forever gone. That would be so wonderful, but it is not the case.

Peter learned of his own nature the hard way. In Matthew 16, Peter had the revelation of the Christ, and then minutes later had a moment of carnality for which Jesus rebuked him harshly. Paul was speaking to the church in 1 Corinthians 3:1-2 and wrote, "I, brethren, could not speak unto you as unto spiritual, but as unto carnal, even as unto babes in Christ. I have fed you with milk, and not with meat: for hitherto ye were not able to bear it, neither yet now are ye able." He was a little bit disturbed. Then he defined the characteristics of carnality, "There is among you envying, and strife, and divisions, are ye not carnal, and walk as men." He was not speaking of gender but rather that they were acting like people of the world or people of darkness. He was saying, "You are acting like this, speaking like this, and doing these things. This should not be so."

The church at Galatia was another very spiritual New Testament church. Paul speaks to the issue of self in

Galatians. He uses the word "flesh." In the use of this word "flesh," he is not talking about the physical body; he is talking about human nature. Flesh is a word that is used interchangeably with "human nature," "carnality," or "fallen nature." In Galatians chapter 5, beginning with verse 19, Paul lists the type of things that self wants to do. If self gets its way, it will commit adultery, fornication, uncleanness, lasciviousness, idolatry, witchcraft, hatred, and variance (which means quarreling and fighting). Self will promote "emulations" (which means to usurp authority). Self brings "wrath and strife and seditions, heresies, envyings, murders, drunkenness, revelings, and such like: of the which I tell you before, as I have told you in times past, that they which do such things shall not inherit the kingdom of God." The kingdom of God is righteousness, joy, and peace in the Holy Ghost. The kingdom of God is the fruit of the Spirit. However, as recorded in Galatians 5:16-17, Paul writes, "Walk in the Spirit and ye shall not fulfill the lust of the flesh" (the desire of self). The flesh, which is the self, "lusteth against the Spirit; and the Spirit against the flesh. And these are contrary the one to the other: so that ye cannot do the things that ye would. But if ye be led of the Spirit, ye are not under the law."

Please see the picture of this struggle for the throne, this wrestling for preeminence. As Barabbas and Jesus stood there, Pilate was effectively saying, "One of these two is going to be crucified." The Apostle Paul used that same phrase in Galatians 2:20, when he said, "I am crucified with Christ." He didn't say that we were to crucify ourselves. I believe self-crucifixion results in self-righteousness. That is the fruit of it, because we would think, "Look what I did. I killed that thing." No, it isn't us killing anything. Paul said, "I am crucified with Christ: nevertheless, I live, yet not I, but Christ liveth in me: and the life which I now live in the flesh." Notice that he said "in the flesh." That means that he is speaking of the here and now, not about heaven. "The life that I now live in the flesh I live by the faith of the Son of God, who loved me, and gave himself for me."

The working of the Holy Spirit can come to us through a dream like the one that Pilate's wife experienced, through the ministry of an angel, or any number of other ways. Angels ministered to Jesus in the garden as He wrestled with self. The strength that we need in the hour of conflict, the help that we need to deal with the issue, is often not a momentary thing. Many times the battle rages for hours, days, months, or even years of our lives. Do not be discouraged if there is something in your life that you know God has been trying to bring to death, yet you still see evidence that it's alive. Don't be discouraged, because God is not going to give up until He finishes that work in you, if you truly want it done.

God is not going to work against your will. If you build a wall and then come up with all kinds of justification for it, it will bring robbery and death. But when the Holy Spirit shows you something, and you desperately want that thing dealt with in your life, He will be faithful to walk you through the process, and it will come to pass.

It's a Process

Don't be discouraged if you have made three trips to the altar or thirty-three. Don't be discouraged if you have prayed all night, fasted for days, and that issue is still there, because there will come a moment of power when it is removed from the throne. We have no idea how deep the roots are until they are finally pulled out. We have no idea of how far we have strayed from God until we start coming back.

Getting self off the throne, moving from carnality to spirituality and from immaturity to maturity, is a process. It's a work of the Holy Spirit. That is why Jesus said we would need the Holy Spirit, not just to tell us which way to go, but to guide us. Jesus said that the Holy Spirit is going to go with us. God could have given us a map, but He gave us something better in a Person. We need Him. Have you ever needed His strength? Have you ever needed His wisdom? We need to pray one for another. We have no idea what someone else is going through or what battles they may be facing. We have no idea the intensity of the war that is going on deep inside. We don't know the severity of their conflict or the depth of their pain, heartache, or loneliness. Jesus had to go to the cross all alone, but He asked the disciples to watch and pray with Him in the garden (Matthew 26:41). They should have been there praying with Him, like Aaron and Hur held up the arms of Moses (Exodus 17:12) in the time of battle. Even though the disciples failed to pray, Jesus still won the battle in the garden. Even if someone disappoints you, even if the church isn't everything you think it ought to be, even if your pastor isn't as spiritual as you think he ought to be, the Holy Spirit is still greater than it all, and God will bring victory.

God is for you. If He puts His finger on something in your life, don't draw back, because He has some good things in mind. Let Him work on you. Ask Him for help. "Father, this self-will of mine is a very ugly monster, and it struggles for its rights. It contends for its place. It insists on its own way. But, Father, I believe your way is better than my way. The greatest desire of my life is to please you. Will you help me deal with this thing? I am being honest with you Father, and I have to tell you the way I feel. If this cup will pass, if there is an easier way, Father, I want that. But please know that it's more important to me that your will be done than mine. And so whatever that means, I yield to you."

Chapter 7

Embracing The Cross

Matthew 16:20-21 records the account of Jesus telling His disciples that He must suffer many things from the elders and chief priests and scribes and be killed and raised again the third day. Peter didn't like that sermon, so he began to rebuke Jesus, essentially saying, "Lord, that can't be" (Matthew 16:22). Peter had left his home and his occupation, and had walked with Jesus for three and a half years. Many people believed that Jesus was going to set up a kingdom upon the earth and overthrow the Roman Empire, so Peter didn't want to hear about Jesus dying. After Peter rebuked Jesus for saying He would be killed, Jesus had to correct him. He turned to Peter and said, "Get thee behind Me Satan: thou are an offence to me: for thou savourest not the things that be of God, but those that be of men" (Matthew 16:23). He in effect said, "There is something coming out of your mouth that is not the Word of the Lord."

It is hard to bring accusation against Peter, because he truly thought that it wouldn't be good for Jesus to die. The disciples loved being around Jesus. He was the answer to everything their hearts desired, so Peter didn't want to think about Him dying. Peter's "self" rose up and said, "No, that shall not be." Jesus, as a result of that exchange, began teaching the disciples in Matthew 16:24 saying, "If any man will come after me, let him deny himself." That word "deny" means "disown or abstain" from self. In effect He said, "If you are going to come after Me, you must deal with self. That is absolutely essential. If you don't deal with self, you can't follow Me. You must then take up your cross and follow Me." First comes dealing with self, then comes taking up the cross. Jesus then said, "Whosoever will save his life shall lose it: and whosoever will lose his life for my sake shall find it." Another translation puts it this way: "Whosoever will live his life for his own sake will lose it. Whosoever will live his life for My sake shall find it. For what is a man profited if he shall gain the whole world and lose his own soul. For what shall a man give in exchange for his soul?"

Luke 9:23 declares, "He said to them all, if any man will come after me, let him deny himself and take up his cross daily, and follow me." Notice that Luke adds the word "daily." Note that daily is not spelled S-u-n-d-a-y. Daily means every day. "For whosoever will save his life shall lose it: but whosoever will lose his life for my sake, the same shall save it. For what is a man advantaged, if he gain the whole world, and lose himself, or be cast away?"

A Challenging Message

This wasn't the only occasion when Jesus preached a tough and challenging message that caused some people to walk away and cease continuing to follow Him. Judas, who was the keeper of the money bag, might have been thinking, "Finally, we are going to get a good offering. With the size of this crowd we are going to balance the budget!" Then Jesus turned around and preached one of those unpopular messages. It's tough to be the treasurer for that kind of an organization. But Jesus wasn't interested in simply accumulating people. He was interested in *changing* people. He wasn't interested in excluding anyone. It is the will of Father than none perish but all come to repentance (2 Peter 3:9). There is nothing wrong with numbers. The book of Acts frequently speaks of numbers. On the day of Pentecost, three thousand were saved. A few days later, five thousand were saved. Acts tells us that believers were added daily to the church. In fact, God put a whole book in the Bible and called it "Numbers."

There is nothing wrong with numbers, but the desire of our Lord is to see changed lives, not just robotic followers. As recorded in Luke 14:26, Jesus said, "If any man come to me, and hate not his father, and mother, and wife, and children, and brethren, and sisters, yea, and his own life also, he cannot be my disciple." This is a controversial scripture, and many people stumble over it. In order to understand it, we must go back to the original Greek word translated "hate." It doesn't mean "despised" as we would normally think. It actually means "love less."

In effect, Jesus was saying, "If any man loves his father or mother more than Me, his priorities are wrong. Unless every man loves Me more than himself, unless I am ahead of self, his priorities are wrong. This is the only order that is acceptable to follow Me. If I am not ahead of self, you will soon not be following Me, because self doesn't want to follow Me."

There are times that we have to say to self, "Be quiet, behave, and fall in line. Self, we are going to follow Jesus. We are going to do what Jesus said. We are going to obey Jesus. Self, you have good ideas, but if they don't line up with Jesus, they are unacceptable." God is not just speaking of avoiding obviously horrible things. Proverbs 14:12 says, "There is a way which seemeth right unto a man, but the end thereof are the ways of death." It means that there is a way that seems right and makes sense, and it is logical, reasonable, and rational. That way is the "self way." Jesus was digging deep when He was teaching them, in effect saying, "If you want to follow Me, you must deal with self. You must deny self. You must confront self. You must acknowledge self for all that it is. And whosoever doesn't bear his cross and come after Me cannot be My disciple." Those are very strong, but important words.

The Cross and the Brazen Altar

The cross has always been central to the plan of God. Going all the way back to the days when God led the children of Israel through the wilderness, we can see the prophetic type of the cross. The way He arranged the tribes and ordered their location was in the form of a cross.

The cross was also typified in the tabernacle. If you were to walk into the tabernacle, you would first encounter the brazen altar and then the brazen laver, which were in the outer court. They were lined up: the brazen altar, then the brazen laver. As you moved into the Holy Place, you would see three pieces of furniture. To the left was the golden candlestick. To the right was the table of shewbread. Then directly ahead was the altar of incense, which was immediately in front of the veil of the Holy of Holies. Inside the Holy of Holies was the ark over which were the cherubim and the glory. If you looked at the configuration of furniture from above, you would see the vertical theme of the cross. So as you moved into the tabernacle, you moved from the foot of the cross to the top of the cross, and the glory was at the head, where Jesus was crowned.

The brazen altar was a very significant part of the furniture in the tabernacle. Its placement was such that no one could go into the tabernacle without encountering the brazen altar. It was the place of sacrifice. As the priest went in, he had to deal with the place of sacrifice before he could move on into the tabernacle. It was the largest item in the tabernacle. In fact, it was so large that all of the other pieces of furniture together could fit inside the brazen altar. It speaks of a great many truths here, because out of the cross, which the brazen altar represents (the place of sacrifice), come all other truths. Everything comes out of the cross. I don't believe there can be any preaching with power unless it is centered on the cross. The cross is God's place of power. In 1 Corinthians 1:18, Paul wrote that, to the unbeliever, the cross is foolishness, but to those who believe, it is the power of God. The cross of Jesus Christ is a vital part of the provision of God.

The cross, represented by the brazen altar, must be encountered as we move into the presence of God. God initially lit the fire on the brazen altar. After that, according to Leviticus chapter 6, the priests had to keep the fire going. Taking fire pans from the fire in the brazen altar, they lit the fires in the Holy Place, the candlestick and the altar of incense. The fire that burned in the altar of incense came out of the fire of the brazen altar. The altar of incense represents praise and worship. There is no genuine praise and worship other than being centered in the cross and in Jesus. In fact, in Revelation chapter 5, the great worship service in heaven shows us worshipping the Lamb. The Lamb of God is on the throne. The Lamb comes from the brazen altar.

This brazen altar represented the cross where Jesus had to go. It was where He gave the final sacrifice, where He gave of Himself, where He died, and where human nature was dealt with. The cross is also representative of the place that you and I have to deal with self. The cross, to Jesus, was the will of the Father. Our cross is the will of the Father. He is not asking us to carry a couple of wooden beams, or the sins of the world. That was Jesus' cross. Our cross is to do the will of the Father. But doing the will of the Father challenges the self-will. That is why, in Gethsemane, we have the beautiful picture of the wrestling between Jesus' human self-will and the will of Father. And so it is with us. Dealing with self, our self-will, is the biggest obstacle to moving into the full expression of the will of God for our lives.

We must understand that the brazen altar and the cross were not pretty sights. We take a cross now and wear it as a piece of jewelry. But the fact of the matter is the cross was not a beautiful place, nor was the brazen altar a beautiful place. The brazen altar was a bloody place. The priests were up to their elbows in blood and guts. The crying of the animals and the smell of burning flesh permeated the area. When we are dealing with self-will and we must bring this self-will into submission to the will of God, it is not pretty. As the fire burns, there is a very unpleasant sight. The closer the fire gets to the flesh, the more it stinks. Jesus said, "You must deal with self. You must deny yourself, and take up your cross. You must take up the will of God for your life daily if you are going to follow Me. Daily! And every time you come to press into God, you must go by the brazen altar." It would have been more pleasant if the priests would have only had to make one trip by the brazen altar, but that wasn't the case. We must keep going back to the altar, because there are times we think our self-will is dead and we find out that it is not. However, the more we put down our self-will, the closer we come to the glory, to the presence of God, to the anointing as we walk in the will of God.

Crucified With Christ

Paul the Apostle, writing in Galatians 2:20, declared, "I am crucified with Christ." He did not say, "I *was*." He said, "I *am* crucified with Christ." He said, "Nevertheless, I live. I am alive. Yet, it isn't me that is alive but the life that I live, I live by the faith of the Son of God who loved me and gave Himself for me." Paul is trying to help us to understand how the life that is within us is the only thing of eternal significance. The human nature that has been passed to us through Adam has to be crucified. It must be crucified in *Christ* at the altar. It's not a case of self-crucifixion because that would only produce self-righteousness. Crucifixion in Christ produces holiness.

As Jesus was hanging there, people that passed by reviled Him. They were mocking Him and doing everything within their power to irritate Him and elicit a response out of His "self." They said, "Thou that destroyest the temple, and buildest it in three days, save thyself. If thou be the Son of God, come down from the cross. Likewise also the chief priests mocking him, with the scribes and elders, said, He saved others; himself he cannot save. If he be the King of Israel, let him now come down from the cross, and we will believe Him" (Matthew 27:40-42). Can you imagine for a moment, the torture, the devious scheme of the enemy, to try to get Jesus to act out of self-will so that He wouldn't fulfill the Father's will? Satan was trying to get Him down from the cross, down from Father's will. The enemy hasn't changed. He does the same thing in our lives. He came to Jesus and tormented Him and said, "You have saved others. You can't even save Yourself. Who do You think You are? If You are really the king, prove it to us."

Jesus could have proven that He was the Son of God. First of all, everything that existed, according to Hebrews 1:3, is held together by the Word of His power. The nails that were in

His hands were held together by the Word of His power, and the cross that He was hanging on was held together by the Word of His power. All He would have had to do was just withdraw that Word and everything would have fallen into ashes.

Secondly, the Scriptures tell us that He could have called more than twelve legions of angels. In the Roman army, a legion was 6,000 men, so twelve legions would be 72,000. In the book of Isaiah, when Sennacherib was going down to destroy Jerusalem during the days of Hezekiah, the Lord sent one angel and he destroyed 185,000 Assyrians. If one angel can kill 185,000, and there are 72,000 angels in 12 legions, then theoretically those 12 legions could collectively kill over 13 billion people. There are over 7 billion people in the world today, but there were only about 300 million in Jesus' day. Jesus could have uttered just one word, and the twelve legions of angels could have wiped out everyone on earth.

Save Yourself!

In effect, the enemy was saying to Jesus, "Call the angels to save yourself. You have that kind of power in your hands. You have that kind of authority in your words." That type of challenge brings a rise in our human nature. The enemy was trying to draw Jesus out of the will of Father, to get Him off the cross. Because Jesus didn't yield, you and I are free. Why didn't He yield? Because He had dealt with self in Gethsemane, though it wasn't easy. He had sweat great drops of blood. It isn't easy to deal with self. "Father, not My will but Thy will be done." Some enemies can even be religious people. People with a religious spirit were trying to get Jesus off the cross. Every drop of blood that fell was shaking hell. I can almost hear the demons screaming, "Stop the blood. Get Him off the cross. It's going to defeat and destroy us." And it did.

Many times when the story of the crucifixion is told, we focus on Jesus' unbearable physical agony, which in itself is beyond our comprehension. But, I believe a major issue was the torment of Jesus' soul being tempted to come out, like the tongue of a serpent, and strike back. Jesus had once said, "Pray for them which despitefully use you" (Luke 6:28). That is an amazing statement. It would have been something if He had said, "Don't despitefully use those that despitefully use you." I mean, just to make things even is quite an accomplishment. But He didn't stop there. He went further and said, "You must pray for them." How can we do that, Jesus? Come on, we are only human. Jesus said, "This is the way. You must deny self. You must pass the brazen altar. You must smell the stench of burning flesh. That is what it costs to follow Me."

Say Yes to Jesus

God has a divine purpose for every one of our lives. He had it before we were born. The problem is that we were born with this flesh garment on us. We have to deal with flesh by denying it and saying, "Flesh, you are not going to get your way." That is not easy. Sometimes I have heard John 3:30 quoted wrongly as saying, "I must decrease and He must increase." That isn't what John the Baptist said. John 3:30 actually says, "He must increase, but I must decrease." That is not just semantics, because the issue is not decreasing ourselves. We would just end up empty. The issue is increasing Him, which results in decreasing self.

How do we deny self? We take up our cross daily. We

choose daily to live for Jesus, to love Jesus, to praise Jesus. We choose daily to live in the Word of God, and to pray to the Lord. When we choose to press into Jesus, self becomes less and less. It isn't sufficient to generate a "hate self" campaign. What we must do is initiate a "love Jesus" campaign. If we would just start loving Him so much that when "self" wants to do something that we know would displease Him, we would say "no" to self, but actually we would be saying "yes" to Jesus. For the victory isn't in saying "no" to self. It is in saying "yes" to Jesus.

About the Author

Blessed with the caring, compassionate heart of a shepherd, Dr. Leonard Gardner has over 60 years of pastoral and ministerial experience. Often called a "pastor's pastor," he has planted churches and mentored pastors and leaders in the true spirit of a "father." Dr. Gardner is the founder of Liberating Word Ministries (www.liberatingword.org) and he travels throughout the United States and abroad with a vision to strengthen and encourage pastors, leaders, churches, and ministries. His heart is for restoration and revival. His style of ministry is seasoned with humor while carrying a powerful anointing. Dr. Gardner has four children and resides in Clinton Township, Michigan.

More Inspirational Books from Dr. Leonard Gardner

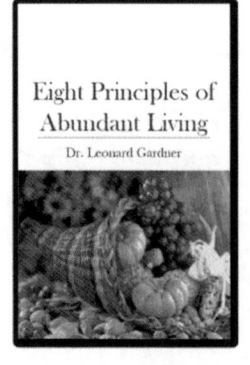

Eight Principles of Abundant Living

In this inspiring and thought provoking book, Pastor Gardner examines each recorded miracle in the Book of John to uncover spiritual principles of abundant living which can lead you into a lifestyle of deep satisfaction, joy, fulfillment, and true happiness.

The Unfeigned Love of God

The Bible uses the word "unfeigned" to characterize the indescribable love of God. Unfeigned means "genuine, real, pure, not pretentious, and not hypocritical." This powerful book, derived from a series of sermons by Pastor Gardner, will help you understand, accept, and embrace the incredible love God seeks to lavish on you.

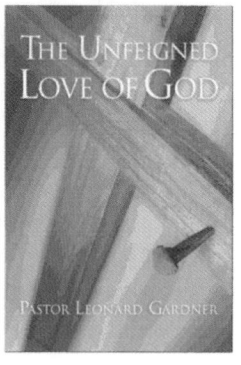

Walking Through the High and Hard Places

Life has its ups and downs. The key to a fulfilling life is learning to "walk through" whatever situation or circumstance you encounter, and to emerge victoriously! The spiritual principles you learn in this book will give you the strength to handle any circumstance in life!

The Work of the Potter's Hands

You are not alive by accident! Isaiah 64:8 declares that God is the potter, and we are the clay. This book examines seven types of Biblical pottery vessels and the process the potter uses to shape and repair vessels. Learn powerful life lessons and know your life is in the hands of a loving God who is forming you through life's experiences so that you "take shape" to fulfill your unique purpose.

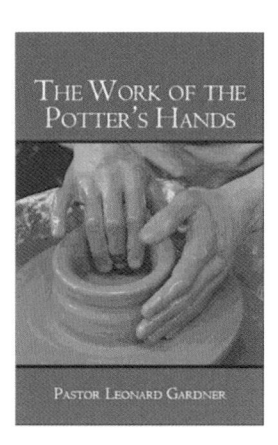

It's All in the Blood

This fascinating book draws intriguing and powerful analogies between the incredible design and operation of blood in the human body, and the life-changing spiritual power and provision that is available in the blood of Jesus Christ.

Like the Eagle

Learn how the eagle's lifestyle and attributes can teach you to "soar higher" in your life, as you become like the eagle in areas such as vision, diet, maturity, renewal, commitment, and living an overcoming life.

The Blood Covenant

Blood covenant is a central theme of the entire Bible, and understanding blood covenant will make the Bible come alive to you in brand new ways. Learn the ten steps of blood covenant, the real significance of communion, the names of God and what they mean, and how walking in a true covenant relationship with God can radically change your life.

Bread that Satisfies

Are you truly satisfied in life? Is your appetite for God everything you desire it to be? The aroma of freshly baked homemade bread awakens hunger in almost anyone. Learn how to stir a similar spiritual hunger in your heart for Jesus, the Bread of Life. Knowing Him will satisfy the deepest hunger of your spirit.

Living in the Favor of God

Is your life is truly blessed? In this study of the Beatitudes, you will learn what Jesus meant by the phrase, "Blessed are they…" Learn the conditions of God's favor as well as the provisions that He has in store for those that desire to truly live a blessed life.

Chosen to Follow Jesus

Who were the twelve disciples? Why did Jesus choose them to follow Him, and what can we learn from their lives? This study of "the twelve" delivers fresh insight into their backgrounds and characteristics, and teaches principles that we, as those chosen to follow Jesus today, can apply to our walk with Him.

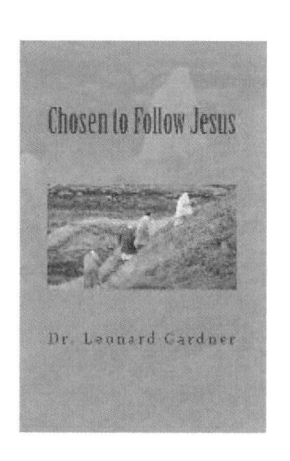

Treasures in the Word
Volume 1

A collection of over 100 "treasures" gleaned from the Bible by Dr. Leonard Gardner over the course of his six decades in ministry, this book is perfect for pastors or teachers searching for fresh sermon ideas, and for those looking for a unique daily devotional book.

Favorites: Best Loved Sermons from 60+ Years of Ministry

This compilation represents a collection of some of Dr. Gardner's sermons that are considered to be among his listeners' favorites. We pray that these powerful messages from the Word of God will encourage, inspire, and draw you closer to Jesus as they have for thousands of eager listeners over the years.

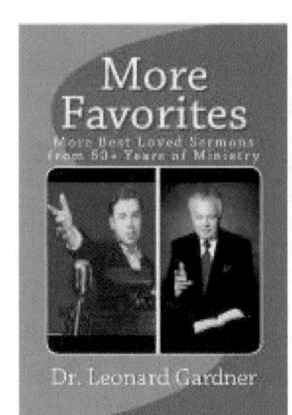

More Favorites: Best Loved Sermons from 60+ Years of Ministry

This second "favorites" compilation represents "more" of Dr. Gardner's sermons that are considered to be among his listeners' favorites.